Praise for

LOST A
FOUN

D1124245

"At this time of great confusion and anxiety about healthcare, patients and their loved ones in America have no more constant, clear-eyed, and committed champions than Dr. Paul Grundy and Dr. Peter Anderson. They've been at that mission for years, and now, in this book, they offer guidance in a friendly form that everyone can use, and should use, to seek and find the care that truly matters and really helps."

— Donald M. Berwick, MD, MPP

Former Administrator of the Centers for Medicare and Medicaid Services; Professor in the Department of Health Policy and Management at Harvard School of Public Health; President Emeritus and Senior Fellow, Institute for Healthcare Improvement

"Healthcare continues to get more complicated, confronting consumers again and again with critical decisions about health insurance, where to go, and how to get what you need from your medical care. There is an urgent need for helpful, unbiased information that isn't selling something. *Lost and Found* provides trustworthy, practical advice on the major decisions that all of us have to make in getting the healthcare we want and need for ourselves and our loved ones."

— Edward H. Wagner, MD, MPH

Group Health Research Institute Senior Investigator Director (Emeritus), MacColl Center, Seattle Washington

"Every family should read *Lost and Found: A Consumer's Guide to Healthcare*. The book tells it like it is, providing '12 Facts of Life' on how the health system works and sometimes doesn't work so well. Most of the book gives detailed advice on how you can get the healthcare you need, and how to make it more affordable. It's a book you'll want to keep forever."

— Thomas Bodenheimer, MD

Professor of Family and Community Medicine, University of California, San Francisco

"Dr. Paul Grundy has been a quiet, unrelenting force driving transformation of primary health care to genuinely provide the majority of people's health needs. I've found that he's someone always worth listening to."

— Atul Gawande, MD, MPH

Surgeon, Brigham and Women's Hospital
Author, "Being Mortal: Medicine and What Matters in the End" and "The Checklist Manifesto"

"Few things in life are as confusing — or as important — as making wise choices about health care. This important book will help you make sense of what's happening and make better choices for you and your family."

— Dr. Elliott S. Fisher MD, MPH

Director of The Dartmouth Institute for Health Policy & Clinical Practice
James W. Squire Professor of Medicine and Community and Family Medicine at the Geisel School of Medicine, Dartmouth

"Thanks to Drs. Anderson and Grundy, we now have a well-written, straightforward, apolitical, consumer-oriented guide for people who want to understand our complex healthcare 'system.'"

— **Michael S. Barr, MD, MBA, FACP**

Executive Vice President, National Committee for Quality Assurance

"Amid the unsettling and confusing complexity of the U.S. health system, including the innumerable provisions of the Affordable Care Act, come the calming and clarifying voices of Drs. Peter Anderson and Paul Grundy. With clarity and common-sense advice, these physician leaders explain how things work and why patients have to partner with their 'familiar' primary care physicians and engage actively in decisions about their care. They paint an optimistic picture that the future of healthcare is bright, and we can't help but believe."

— **Vivian S. Lee, MD, PhD, MBA**

CEO University of Utah Health Care, Dean School of Medicine

"This is a refreshing contribution to the world of publications discussing the challenges of navigating our complex healthcare system. The authors provide very real and practical strategies to get high quality and lower cost healthcare in the United States, with a familiar physician and patient-centered medical home prepared to meet their needs."

— **J. Nwando Olayiwola, MD, MPH, FAAFP**

Director, Center for Excellence in Primary Care
Associate Professor, Department of Family and Community Medicine
University of California, San Francisco
San Francisco General Hospital

"Read this book! Directed to 'non-medical' people, it is also useful to health professionals. Anderson and Grundy provide the clearest, most concise description I have seen of the state of health care today. They argue convincingly that everyone should have a *familiar physician*. They provide clear paths to navigate the healthcare financing maze. They also offer detailed, specific resources for people in special circumstances such as lack of health insurance, and offer sound practical advice about how all of us can succeed in managing our own health."

— Michael K. Magill, MD
Professor and Chairman, Department of Family and Preventive Medicine
University of Utah School of Medicine

"*Lost and Found* picks up where *The Familiar Physician* left off, offering powerful evidence of how data will transform healthcare and make it truly personal again. For caregivers, the ability to better understand population health of patients and their communities will revolutionize care. We are fortunate to have the combined expertise of Dr. Anderson and Dr. Grundy to guide us on this journey toward better outcomes for patients."

— Daniel S. Pelino
General Manager, Global Public Sector
IBM Corporation

"*Lost and Found* provides a no-nonsense, plain-language guide to the complex world of healthcare, from the value of a personal physician to gaining better outcomes for you and your family at lower out-of-pocket costs. This is a must-read for the informed consumer of healthcare in the US."

— Bruce Bagley, MD
Past president of the American Academy of Family Physicians and former president and CEO of TransforMED

"A clear and comprehensive guide to obtaining high quality and affordable healthcare from two of the leading experts in the field of primary care medicine."

— James Lloyd Michener, MD

Chair and Professor of Community and Family Medicine, Duke University School of Medicine

"*Lost and Found* highlights the importance of the technology-enabled, patient-centered, primary healthcare team to achieve America's goal of better care for all. It's a wakeup call for patients and providers alike."

— Stephen M. Shortell, PhD, MBA, MPH

Blue Cross of California Distinguished Professor of Health Policy and Management and Director, Center for Healthcare Organizational and Innovation Research (CHOIR)
Dean Emeritus
School of Public Health
UC-Berkeley

"Having dealt with a hospitalization of my wife and an ER visit with my mother over a five-day period showed me the importance of this guide. I cannot imagine being a consumer without the knowledge that *Lost and Found* offers with regard to our healthcare system. Even for a physician like me providing support to my family, it can be hard to navigate."

— Joseph S. Miller, MD

2015 Family Physician of the Year
President Nebraska AFP

"Paul Grundy and Peter Anderson have been stalwart and inspiring leaders in the quest for better primary care in America. They have each, in their own way, modeled team building, empowered creative people around the country and remained steadfast in their commitment to better patient care through stronger primary care. In that quest, much of which is described in this book, Drs. Grundy and Anderson focused on what is best in medicine, and we all owe them a debt of gratitude."

—Richard J. Baron, MD, MACP
President and CEO, American Board of Internal Medicine

Lost and Found:
A Consumer's Guide to Healthcare
by
Peter B. Anderson, MD and Paul H. Grundy, MD
with Tom Emswiller and Bud Ramey

© Copyright 2015 Peter B. Anderson, MD and Paul H. Grundy, MD
with Tom Emswiller and Bud Ramey

Line illustrations: Mark R. Shaw

ISBN 978-1-63393-186-2

Published by

 köehlerbooks™

210 60th Street
Virginia Beach, VA 23451
212-574-7939
www.koehlerbooks.com

LOST AND FOUND

A Consumer's Guide
to Healthcare

Peter B. Anderson, MD
and Paul H. Grundy, MD

with Tom Emswiller and Bud Ramey

VIRGINIA BEACH
CAPE CHARLES

Dedication

This book is dedicated to everyone who sets out on the journey toward better health. Our hope is that it will be a guidepost along the way.

Table of Contents

Acknowledgements

THE DEVELOPMENT OF THIS book has been a team effort. I'm thankful for the expertise, the effort, and the real enthusiasm each person brought to the process. Usually, writing tends to be a one-person activity, but in this case it was very collaborative and for that I'm grateful. This book wouldn't be what it is without the work of this team, and I certainly wouldn't have had the same pleasure while writing it.

First, I want to thank my wife Laurie, who never stopped believing in the value of a familiar physician. Your companionship and love for nearly 40 years have formed the setting in which this book could be written. Your motivation, ideas, and perspective have been critical to *Lost and Found*.

Next, thanks to Hannah Teague, a fellow employee at Team Care Medicine, whose ability to understand healthcare issues and communicate to readers in a relevant way has been essential to the creation of this book. I'm deeply grateful for the endless hours you spent writing, researching, editing, and contributing to this material.

Thanks to Dr. Mark Shaw for making our ideas come alive through your illustrations. Your leadership, friendship, and support over the past five years have been so encouraging and much needed along the way.

Many people gave of their valuable time and expertise, and we'd like to thank them for their contributions to this book: Dr. Bruce Bagley, George Clark, Dr. Jack Cochran, Dr. Michael Fine, Malcolm Gladwell, Joe Grundy, Dr. Kevin Hopkins, Anne Hutchens, Walter Kmetz, Craig Nuckles, Dr. Drew O'Neal, the Patient Advocate Foundation, Rick Pearce, Dr. Debra Scammon, Erin Singleton, Michelle Sunderland, Dr. Eric Topol, and Andrew Webber.

My staff at Hilton Family Practice who for more than 25 years were invaluable in helping me see what good care should look like while supporting our ability to provide it. Their care and their caring for the people we served, and their skills, expertise and humanity, are an essential part of why this book now exists—and I miss working with them very much.

And lastly, thanks to everyone who works at Team Care Medicine. You have all sacrificed and worked tirelessly to bring this dream of robust primary care closer to reality. This book would never have happened without your energy, skill, and dedication.

—Dr. Peter Anderson

In the creation of this book as in all of my work and life experiences, I am indebted to my family for their enduring support while living with me though turmoil in Sierra Leone and Yemen, revolution in the former USSR, and upheaval in South Africa while gracefully adjusting to diverse cultures and situations in South Korea, Singapore, and Saudi Arabia. I also wish to acknowledge and thank the following friends, colleagues and sources of inspiration:

Thomas Bodenheimer, MD, MPH and Kevin Grumbach, MD, who long have championed a more just, progressive and consumer-centered version of primary care medicine in their roles within the Department of Family and Community Medicine at the University of California at San Francisco.

Susan Baker, MPH and Timothy Baker, MD, MPH for mentoring me in their pioneering work in population/public health and preventive care at Johns Hopkins.

Michael Magill, MD and Vivian Lee, MD, PhD at the University of Utah School of Medicine; Charles Kilo, MD in Portland, Oregon; Joseph Scherger, MD, MPH, Clinical Professor of Family Medicine at the University of Southern California; Ed Wagner, MD, MPH, MacColl Institute for Healthcare Innovation, Seattle; and Daniel Duffy, MD, former dean of the Oklahoma University School of Community Medicine who believe in the kind of accessible and integrated healthcare we talk about in this book and keep reminding us that it can exist and thrive.

Bob Kocher, MD, Elizabeth Fowler, PhD, JD, Kavita Patel, MD and William (Billy) Wynne, JD for their passion for health reform and their skills in translating language into law — and Richard Gilfillan, MD, Ted Wymyslo, MD, Richard Baron, MD, and Craig A. Jones, MD who helped implement the law through innovative pilot programs and state health reform initiatives.

Leaders in the health plan industry like Jill Hummel, JD, Thomas Simmer, MD, Julie Schilz, BSN, MBA, and Sam Nussbaum, MD who helped develop provider payment models that reward improved quality, better health outcomes, patient safety, and access.

Andrew Morris-Singer, MD and Marci Nielsen, PhD, MPH for their roles in primary care revitalization and innovation through education, clinical practice, and community advocacy.

My teachers and mentors including Philip Lee, MD, Peter Budetti, MD, JD, Lawrence McHargue, PhD, Ralph Crandall, PhD, and Don Lorance, PhD.

My bosses and amazing mentors in diplomacy and foreign service including Ambassador Thomas Pickering, Ambassador Robert Strauss, Consulate General F. Allen "Tex" Harris, Ambassador Genta Holmes, Ambassador Andrew Winter, Ambassador William Rugh, Ambassador Melissa Wells, Ambassador James Collins, Ambassador Theodore Kattouf, Deputy Assistant Secretary of State Allen Keiswetter, and Ambassador Shirley Temple Black.

Dan Pelino, Sean Hogan, and Randy MacDonald who have championed IBM's vision of global healthcare and supported efforts to transform primary care to make it more responsive to IBM employees and all consumers, while also taking the time to empower me in my work over the past decade.

The thousands of "Familiar Physicians" and other primary care providers throughout America who are working every day to build trusting relationships with their patients and deliver more accessible, consumer-centered care.

Finally, I want to acknowledge and thank, in countless ways, the healthcare consumers who are active partners in the kind of care that once was lost but now is found. We hope you enjoy reading about the ongoing journey toward improved care, less confusion, and lower costs as much as we enjoyed writing about it.

—Dr. Paul Grundy

Foreword

WE HAVE A LOVE-HATE relationship with our healthcare system, and the "love" part is no mystery. We enjoy the world's most technologically advanced resources, sophisticated interventions, and highly trained medical specialists. Our level of emergency and trauma care is unequaled. When it comes to accommodating people with disabilities, carrying out research, or developing drugs for rare diseases, few do it better.

So what's not to love? Well, to begin with, the costs are overwhelming. Paying more for our care than anyone else in the world would seem like a fair tradeoff, except for the inconvenient fact that our life expectancy is lower than virtually all other developed nations. This crushing expense may be an inevitable part of a technology-based health system that's fragmented, wasteful, and set up to pay for volume rather than quality. But in the meantime, it's threatening the financial security of growing numbers of individuals, families, and businesses.

When you add the difficulty that millions of Americans experience trying to gain timely access to primary care, include our high rate of chronic disease, and then throw in a recent report in the Mayo Clinic Proceedings indicating that many long-accepted medical procedures aren't really doing much good, it's easy to understand the source of all the frustration and dissatisfaction.

Beyond the statistics and facts, however, there's something

even more troubling that can best be described as a sense of loss — a loss of momentum in moving toward a healthcare system that better serves the people who rely on it without creating financial hardship on a personal and national level. And even worse, a loss of hope that what lies ahead will be an improvement over what exists now.

The good news in the story of American healthcare is that we've found something that's beginning to energize the people who provide care, the people who receive it, and the people who pay for it. And it's focused on a growing ability to move from passive acceptance of a broken healthcare system to active participation in making it better. Toward that objective, this book was created to help you improve the way you use and pay for healthcare, not only for the purpose of saving money, but also for being able to make informed choices for you and your loved ones that lead to better health.

The information that follows can help you navigate the obstacles that stand between you and high-quality, affordable healthcare. You'll read about why primary care, more than any other aspect of medicine, will determine the quality of our healthcare as a nation. Along the way you'll get a close-up view of one of the essential elements in healthcare reform, the Patient-Centered Medical Home. You'll see the value inherent in a strong patient-physician relationship and how a "familiar physician" delivers the best preventive and acute care and chronic care management. You'll learn how skilled healthcare teams, partnering with you as an essential member, can provide the right care at the right time in the right place. And you'll find out how to save money without sacrificing quality in today's changing healthcare environment.

Your guides on this journey of discovery are Dr. Peter Anderson and Dr. Paul Grundy, two physicians who bring a unique combination of personal experience and expertise to the quest for affordable and effective healthcare. Over the past decade, their tireless and innovative efforts on behalf of primary care medicine have received national recognition in both the medical and business communities. Their commitment to sharing that experience and restoring primary care to the foundation of American medicine is the basis of this book.

A FEW WORDS ABOUT THE IMAGES

You'll also see some illustrations throughout this book. We've integrated them into the narrative for two primary reasons. The first is to employ author Dan Roam's model of "vivid thinking," or visual and verbal interdependence. This combination of simple pictures and words to communicate ideas is particularly helpful when delving into a complex topic.

Second, you've probably heard a lot about healthcare, but after a while all those words can make you want to tune out. But we believe it's more important than ever for you to understand what's happening in healthcare and how those changes affect you and your family. And sometimes we need to see, hear, read—and yes, even draw—to think differently and find creative solutions.

We all need to begin a fresh conversation around healthcare in order to move forward. So these images are far from an attempt to oversimplify an inherently multifaceted subject or to force a one-size-fits-all approach. They're used with the intent to explain serious, important topics in a clear, innovative way and help you become more engaged in making the right choices for your health.

KEEPING POLITICS OUT OF HEALTHCARE
. . . AT LEAST IN THIS BOOK

Much of the information we get about healthcare these days comes filtered through the ideology and strategies of both major political parties. So if you're wondering where politics fit into this book, the simple answer is that they don't. Taking a political position around health and the social, cultural, and, ultimately, very human issues involved does little to enlighten us on either the problems or the solutions. Our decision was to leave politics at the door with the hope that you'll do the same in order to better focus on what's important—the future of healthcare and its impact on our personal health and that of our families and communities.

Eight Steps to Becoming a Better Healthcare Consumer

WE COULD ALL USE some direction for the road ahead in order to save money and find the right healthcare. Whether you're managing healthcare costs for yourself, your family, or the employees who work for your business, these eight steps will help you make successful decisions:

1. Find and keep a familiar physician
2. Encourage your familiar physician's practice to become a medical home (if it's not already)
3. Use the appropriate preventive screenings your provider offers
4. Understand insurance plans and select which is the best fit for you and your family
5. Shop for healthcare procedures and pharmaceuticals
6. Understand what the future of healthcare looks like
7. Challenge unreasonable charges and bills
8. Navigate the best resources for assistance if you're underinsured or uninsured

Despite what you may think, it's possible to get high-quality, low-cost healthcare in America. And this book will help you find it.

Chapter 1

AMERICAN HEALTHCARE'S 12 FACTS OF LIFE

"SPACE," READS THE INTRODUCTION to *The Hitchhiker's Guide to the Galaxy*, "is big. Really big. You just won't believe how vastly, hugely, mind-bogglingly big it is. And so on." That tongue-in-cheek description could almost be used to explain the field of medicine. The last several decades of research and intervention have yielded more discovery and progress than ever before while greatly expanding the scope of medical possibility.

Thanks to remarkable advances in technology, increased knowledge of the intricacies of the human mind and body, huge strides in diagnostic and treatment strategies, and extensive pharmaceutical development, an explanation of how healthcare has changed in recent years can be fairly lengthy. And while doctors and researchers may not want to dwell on the potentially negative side of medical progress, the truth is that all this innovation has also helped create a healthcare system that's increasingly more complex, inconvenient, and expensive.

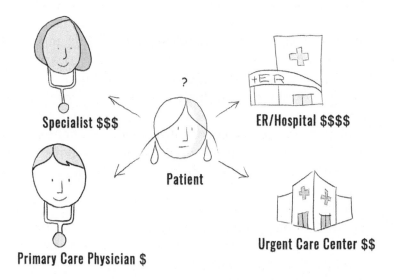

Specialist $$$

ER/Hospital $$$$

Patient

Urgent Care Center $$

Primary Care Physician $

It's overly complex because of the often necessary but nonetheless overwhelming body of regulations that surround healthcare, the turf wars that can exist between and among administrative and clinical staff, and the baffling array of insurance and reimbursement options in place.

The inconvenience is an unavoidable part of an approach which, despite the growing efforts toward centering care delivery around the patient, still revolves around the needs of medical providers, who operate predominantly out of a set location with limited hours.

As for expenses, let's get a sense of scope before we consider how things got that way:

Healthcare currently consumes about 18% of the Gross National Product (GNP) in the United States. To give you some perspective on how that figure has increased, it was just 5% in 1960. What that means in the big picture is that we disburse a larger percentage of our national spending on healthcare than on shelter, food, and clothing put together. For a comparison, we spend 2.5 times more per family than the average of the other economically developed nations in the world.

On a personal level, this burden is beginning to translate (and already has for many people) into higher out-of-pocket expenses for copays and deductibles, as well as higher health insurance rates at best and insufficient or non-existent coverage at worst. When the costs of healthcare are transferred to employers through increased rates for providing insurance coverage to employees, the cost of everything else goes up, too.

The reasons behind the crippling expense include everything from high prescription drug prices, excessive administrative costs, and a legal system that forces doctors to practice defensive medicine to the for-profit component embedded in our healthcare system and many Americans' rejection of restrictions on the kinds of lifestyle choices and behaviors that lead to disease and disability. And the list goes on.

While the complex and interrelated factors that influence the high cost of our nation's healthcare can all be improved, it will take time and a lot of wrangling between the vested interests that are involved. But one of the principal causes of expensive healthcare on which we can make a more immediate impact is our less-than-optimal access to primary care.

Whether patients are insured, underinsured, or uninsured, not being able to see a primary care physician in a timely manner or not having the coverage or financial ability to do so has led to increasing numbers of urgent care and emergency room visits as well as hospital admissions. Lack of access has also resulted in treatment that's deferred to a time when the condition moves from minor to serious. All of these options are considerably more expensive than simply getting in to see a doctor when you first experience a problem.

In fact, the issue of primary care access forms the core of these "12 Facts of Life" we compiled to sum up some of the concerns related to healthcare that are likely to have a direct impact on you:

1. When people get sick or injured unexpectedly, they're seldom able to see their own doctor because appointments may not be available on short notice.

2. Appointments are typically rushed, and the provider is often more focused on entering medical record data into the computer than communicating directly with the patient.

3. For the sake of convenience and sometimes even necessity, patients end up in urgent or emergency care and see a doctor they've never met, pay much more, and often receive unnecessary (and expensive) tests.

4. The aging population of Baby Boomers threatens to overwhelm primary care providers because of the time needed to handle the complexity of their medical conditions. Many older people have multiple chronic conditions as they advance in years.

5. Due to the poor access to primary care, almost 50% of adults with chronic diseases aren't getting adequate treatment, and about 45% of all healthy adults aren't getting recommended care. This lack of chronic care management and preventive tests leads to much higher expenses later when conditions become severe and require a higher level of care.

6. Our healthcare system is oriented toward treatment rather than prevention. More than 40% of American deaths are due to lifestyle issues and are therefore essentially preventable. Life expectancy in the U.S. is ranked 38th out of all industrialized nations.

7. Businesses struggle with the high costs of providing healthcare benefits to their employees. This expense has become the largest sector of the entire American economy and is stunting job development.

8. The multitude of public and private insurance systems is complicated and confusing to healthcare providers as well as patients.

9. Hospital systems build state-of-the-art facilities, but a high percentage of people can't afford to go to them.

10. On the other hand, because hospitals must provide 24/7, full emergency response to anyone who comes through their doors, regardless of ability to pay, costs shift to the businesses, people, and third party payers who can. Fees add up quickly, and as an example, the

average ER bill for a person showing symptoms of what turns out to be a common cold has climbed to $800-$1,200.

11. Uninsured people must often rely on the ER for free primary care. Unable to afford health insurance costs (which have generally increased every year for the last decade), they jump into the safety net of the ER to get the care they need—at around 10 times the cost of a primary care physician.

12. Our high-cost medical care is the single greatest cause of bankruptcy proceedings for individuals and has a similarly negative effect on businesses, states, and the nation.

HOT WATER AND HARD QUESTIONS

We all know the old story about how, if a frog is placed in boiling water, it will immediately jump out. Place the same frog in cool water, however, and gradually, almost imperceptibly turn up the heat, and it will accommodate the slow but steady change and end up being boiled. As it turns out, the story is a myth. The frog, despite its cold-blooded nature will, in fact, get out of the water when it becomes uncomfortably warm.

The premise behind the story may be false, but it's always been a great metaphor for illustrating how failure to respond to gradual threats or negative changes will eventually land you in a bad place. To a certain extent, that's what has happened with many Americans who've become habituated to the facts of life we've just mentioned and other unsatisfactory aspects of our healthcare system. Many people simply accept the state of care that has continued to become more and more inadequate over time.

But unlike the proverbial frog, a growing number of people are starting to respond to the heat. As we travel around the country working with businesses and physician groups, and especially while talking with healthcare consumers, we're hearing some of the same thoughts from these individuals who are frustrated but want to believe there's a better system than the one their questions reflect:

- *Why can't my doctor be more accessible and accommodating when I need an appointment?*
- *What is the "right" medical care, and how would I know it when I experience it?*
- *How can I get personalized and reliable information to help make decisions about my family's health?*
- *How do I choose the right insurance plan for my family?*
- *Why is healthcare so expensive, and can I ever expect it to be more affordable?*
- *Is it reasonable to equate expensive care with the best care?*

Our experience has taught us there's no easy or immediate solution to create a vastly improved system for the people who use, provide, and pay for healthcare. But we believe we must take these and related questions head on, then find and share answers. That's what we'll be doing in the following pages with the hope that when you finish this book, you'll be ready to navigate your way to the kind of healthcare you deserve.

And like Arthur Dent, the fictional character in *The Hitchhiker's Guide* who wandered through the universe, any person who can traverse the length and breadth of our healthcare system, struggle against the odds, and come out on the other side better prepared to choose the right care is clearly a consumer to be reckoned with.

Chapter 2:

THE VALUE OF A FAMILIAR PHYSICIAN

THERE ARE OVER SEVEN billion people in the world, and just about every one of them is in at least one type of important relationship. The sheer number of human connections is astounding. But when you think about it, all relationships can essentially be separated into two categories: the good ones and the bad ones.

The bad ones tend to be bad for a diverse and infinitely complex range of reasons. But when you drill down on the good relationships, you generally find a small number of universal characteristics that include things like honest communication, trust, and common purpose. Keep those attributes in mind as we look at why a familiar physician can play such a vital role in improving and maintaining your health.

WHERE EVERYBODY KNOWS YOUR NAME

As you would guess from the term, what we mean when we talk about a "familiar physician" is a primary care doctor with whom you have an established relationship. Her or his competency, knowledge of medicine, and ability to provide appropriate care represent the starting point. After that, the value of familiar physicians is that they know their patients beyond the purely physical level and understand how emotional, psychosocial, and economic factors, along with family dynamics and current circumstances, can have a significant influence on a person's health.

There's also mutual trust between the physician and patient that helps assure clear communication and an honest, two-way exchange of information. Research shows that patients who have an established history with their physicians tend to relax more during appointments and communicate more truthfully and accurately about their health. The result is an improved information transfer between patient and provider. This superior dialogue and the trust that goes with it leads to more accurate diagnoses, more effective implementation of treatment strategies, and better patient lifestyle decisions. Familiar physicians who have a whole-person perspective are also more likely to correctly diagnose the cause of certain medical problems such as headache, abdominal pain, fatigue, and shortness of breath, which can sometimes have emotional or psychological roots.

Decision-making, once the exclusive domain of the provider, can become a collaborative activity between the doctor and patient. When difficult, costly, or invasive next steps are needed, it's much easier for a patient to rely on his or her familiar physician to advise the right course of treatment. Both are involved in the discussions and choices regarding treatment options and expectations, as well as potentially negative side effects.

In some cases, the "side effects" may include those created by the immediate sticker shock and the longer-term financial concerns people may experience when they're exposed to high out-of-pocket costs and less comprehensive coverage for their healthcare. A familiar physician, a doctor who approaches your care from a position of wholeness and continuity rather than from the perspective of a single encounter, is far more likely to discuss the financial implications of treatment alternatives.

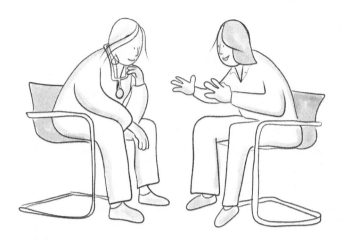

BUILDING THE BRIDGE TO BETTER OUTCOMES

The trust and understanding that develop between you and your familiar physician can give you far more than just a feeling of comfort. Numerous studies show that patients experience better health outcomes when they have an ongoing relationship with their physician. Results are improved for chronic conditions like diabetes, hypertension, congestive heart failure, asthma, and COPD. Patients avoid many of the complications and expenses that arise from unmanaged health issues. Studies also show there's an increased use of preventive screenings and services, fewer ER and hospital admissions, and a noteworthy decrease in mortality. And patients' total costs of care are lower.

Part of the reason for these improved outcomes is the fact that people with a consistent relationship with one doctor are more highly motivated to comply with their physician's advice in general and with prescribed medications or recommendations in particular.

At the same time, the familiar physician becomes your foremost advocate. Although most physicians would hopefully make the special effort required to treat a patient in need, the impetus to do so quickly (even when it means making some major scheduling adjustments) is one of the benefits of a relationship that develops over time. The following story, which we'll share in Dr. Anderson's own words, offers a good example:

One morning I was in the hallway of my practice, about to enter an exam room, when my nurse approached and told me one of our patients, Kristen, had called the office in severe pain and wanted an appointment as quickly as possible. All of the slots (including the urgent ones) were already filled, the rest of our schedule was booked for the day, and it wasn't clear when we could see Kristen. What both my nurse and I knew, however, was that Kristen had given birth only six days earlier.

It took just a moment to assess the urgency of Kristen's need. She'd been my patient for five years, and I wanted to do whatever I could to alleviate her pain— especially because she had a newborn and was already experiencing a range of new challenges. And because she and I had developed a good patient-doctor relationship, I also knew that she wouldn't describe a situation as urgent unless it actually was. I told Donna to bring her in immediately, and less than an hour later we saw her and did a minor procedure on a large cyst related to her delivery. It took about a minute to make the incision and drain it, providing her with instant relief.

Kristen will never forget that day. And I won't either. Turning away patients in need and sending them to urgent care or the ER to endure long waits and costly procedures isn't why I became a physician. The satisfaction of caring for Kristen and preventing any further suffering was an extension of our mutual trust and past experience, and easily worth the inconvenience of juggling schedules and working a little later.

LIFE WITHOUT A FAMILIAR PHYSICIAN

On the other side of the coin, imagine a scenario in which every time you're sick, you feel like you're a stranger in an unfamiliar place, enduring long waits for someone to diagnose and treat you—someone who may never have seen you before and probably won't see you again. That's because almost half of all acute health interventions take place outside the context of an established doctor-patient relationship. Even patients with a regular primary care doctor—a familiar physician—don't expect to see the person they refer to as "my doctor" if they need to be seen on an urgent basis like the woman in Dr. Anderson's story.

If your primary care practice, assuming that you have one, can't give you relatively fast access to care, there's a good chance you'll head for an urgent care center or the ER. Another possibility now available in many areas is the local pharmacy where nurse practitioners and physician assistants do tests, make diagnoses, and write prescriptions. There are also walk-in clinics in some big-box retail stores now. In addition, you can get consultations and webcam-assisted diagnoses and treatments online for a number of common conditions.

The fact is that under certain circumstances—and with appropriate expectations—each of these options can provide some degree of health benefit as well as convenience. But none of them is a substitute for the ongoing, personalized, and comprehensive care you receive from a doctor who sees you as more than a medical record, a data set, or an unknown person with a problem. None of them have a sense of you as a whole person or will focus on your total physical, emotional, and mental wellbeing. None of these options can coordinate all the care you may need from a single, central place. And none of them come with a familiar physician.

A SON TALKS ABOUT A FAMILIAR PHYSICIAN FOR HIS MOTHER

One of our colleagues, Dr. Eric J. Topol, a noted cardiologist, geneticist, researcher, and author of *The Patient Will See You Now,* recently interviewed journalist Malcolm Gladwell, best-selling author of *The Tipping Point, Blink, Outliers, What the Dog Saw* and *David and Goliath.* In this portion of their exchange, which included thoughts about new types of doctors entering medicine, Mr. Gladwell describes what his elderly mother most wants and needs out of our healthcare system. Dr. Topol kindly gave us permission to include part of the discussion in this book, and we believe it represents an excellent summation, and a very personal perspective, on the familiar physician.

Malcolm Gladwell: *"What does my mother want from the medical profession? She uses far more of the healthcare profession than I do. Her needs are much greater than mine, which is typical.*

What she really wants is an individual physician in her life who knows her well, who listens to her, whom she trusts, and with whom she can periodically have extended conversations. That is what she wants. It matters less to her that she has access to world-class, cutting-edge technology, because she is 85.

She wants someone who can guide her through what is becoming an increasingly complicated, confusing, and terrifying period in her life. She doesn't just need someone capable of having those conversations with her. She needs a system that allows that physician to spend 25 minutes with my mother when she needs 25 minutes, which is not every time she goes. Maybe it is just twice a year, but right now we have a system where finding 25 minutes twice a year is really hard.

So we can change who we select for medicine all we want, but unless we change the nature of medical practice, it is pointless. We are just going to have brilliantly gifted doctors capable of having these kinds of discussions who instead are forced into a system where they have got to run the patients through an electronic treadmill."

(Used with permission from MedScape: medscape.com/viewarticle/847711.)

START GETTING FAMILIAR

The benefits of building a strong relationship with your primary care doctor are well documented in terms of staying healthier, managing illness, and preventing disease. If you don't have a familiar physician, now is the time to find one, because as with all relationships, getting to know one another takes some time. With more people gaining health insurance through the Affordable Care Act, and with an even greater shortage of primary care doctors very likely to come down the road, put this book down and find a doctor (if you don't already have one) who fits your needs.

Along with the sense of urgency on beginning the search, take time to choose carefully, factoring in everything from insurance restrictions, location, and training to gender, age, and philosophy of care. For example, some doctors may be quicker than others to refer you to a specialist or prescribe antibiotics rather than take a watchful waiting approach. Thanks to a variety of online "report cards" and other resources, there's much more information available that can help you choose a physician.

It's perfectly appropriate to interview a physician before making a choice (if the physician has openings for this). In fact, the best time to evaluate someone for the possible position of your familiar physician is before you actually have a health concern or a preventive care need. If you do conduct an interview, be sure to ask the kinds of questions that will help you make a decision, including when the physician intends to retire. This is a valid question for you if you're looking to take a first step in what hopefully will be a long journey together.

Keep in mind that a familiar physician may be the most valuable professional relationship you'll ever have, seeing you through many of the stages and transitions of your life. Based on a considerable body of research, you're more likely to live longer, live healthier, and spend less for medical care when you see your familiar physician on a long-term basis. No other single entity in medicine can help you achieve those outcomes. That's why seeing your familiar physician, both when you're sick and well, is the most important thing you can do for your health.

Chapter 3:

THERE'S NO PLACE LIKE THE MEDICAL HOME

THERE'S NO DOORBELL TO ring, and you won't find a comfortable family room or a well-equipped kitchen. Despite the use of the word "home" and the many images that it brings to mind, the medical home isn't a physical structure or a specific location. It's a relatively new approach to healthcare that relies on comprehensive and coordinated primary care delivered through a high-performing team. And the medical home is the ideal setting for the care you'll receive from the familiar physician we've been discussing.

While the medical home doesn't depend upon a physical building—though it does integrate your primary care office into the equation—it definitely offers a sense of place. For example, it's where you call when your child's fever won't go down, when your spouse has recurring heartburn, or when you need help managing your high blood pressure. It's where your familiar physician practices, where the diagnostic test you need is ordered to figure out the problem with your knee, and where you can get a referral to the specialist who can treat it with an innovative surgical procedure. It's also the source of the advice you or your loved one needs when deciding quality of life is more important than the strain of another treatment with little possibility of benefit.

You get the idea. It's the first place to which you and your family turn to maintain your health and treat illness or injury when it occurs, across the full spectrum of care. When it's working well, it's where your wants, needs, and preferences are acknowledged and respected and where you can expect the education and support needed to make informed decisions and participate more fully in your own care.

A high-functioning medical home also encourages the flow of information and services between your familiar physician and specialists, hospitals, home health, long-term care, and other providers when necessary. Dynamic medical homes, closely coordinated with all other healthcare providers through a practice-based care team, are the best place to find effective and affordable care. It's where your medical care begins and where most of it is received. At the same time it serves as your "hub" and coordination point for healthcare received outside of the primary medical home.

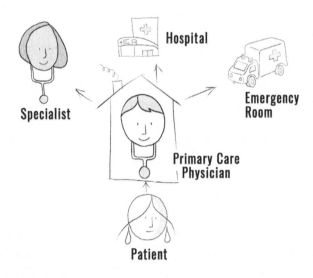

A SHORT HISTORY OF THE MEDICAL HOME

The medical home may not be an actual building, but it does have a solid foundation. In 1967, the medical home concept began when the leadership of the American Academy of Pediatrics (AAP) defined it as an archiving system for children's medical records. At that time its primary focus was related to caring for children with special healthcare needs. Thirty-five years later in 2002, the AAP expanded the medical home concept to include the creation of "accessible, continuous, comprehensive, family-centered, coordinated, compassionate, and culturally-effective care."

Business became involved with the medical home in 2005 when IBM realized rising healthcare costs in the United States were threatening its future as a multinational corporation. Around that time, based on the belief that the most effective and efficient health system would result from strengthening primary care and the Patient-Centered Medical Home, IBM led the way to bring together a diverse group of stakeholders that represented healthcare providers, insurers, employers, and individuals.

This group, which is now the Patient-Centered Primary Care Collaborative (PCPCC), partners with the American Academy of Family Physicians, the American Academy of Pediatrics, the American College of Physicians, and the American Osteopathic Association to promote the medical home as a transformative agent in American healthcare and the crucial building block to an effective primary care system.

IBM's work, combined with the efforts of the Collaborative and the physician-led organizations mentioned above, has played a major role in reaffirming the role of robust primary care while also bringing the medical home into the forefront of health reform. (The full story of the development of the medical home can be found in our book *The Familiar Physician*.)

Politically, the medical home is endorsed by members of both major parties and has received bipartisan support from Congressional leaders over the past decade. The aims and actual elements of the medical home also appear in the heavily studied state of Massachusetts healthcare reform legislation, as well as in the Affordable Care Act.

THE SEVEN PRINCIPLES OF THE
PATIENT-CENTERED MEDICAL HOME

In 2007, seven core features were agreed upon by the primary care organizations mentioned above to define the necessary functions of a medical home. These features also define what's needed for individual patients to cost-effectively maximize their health outcomes by utilizing the medical home—the place where you find the familiar physician and more.

Principle #1: a personal physician

Patients choose and keep the same primary care doctor (a familiar physician) on a long-term basis, developing a strong patient-physician bond.

Principle #2: a physician-directed care team

The physician is supported by a clinical team with specialized primary care skills. The result is a patient-centered rather than a physician-centered experience. Dr. Bruce Bagley, former CEO for TransforMed, explains it this way: "It's no longer realistic to expect one person to provide everything for you. The top doctor from the top medical school doing her or his own thing will not get as good a result as the doctor who creates a true team that works in a systematic place with shared responsibility." A high-performing team always exceeds the capacity of high-performing individuals.

Principle #3: whole person orientation

The physician and his or her clinical team focus on the "whole" patient, not only on a particular medical condition or diagnosis. In other words, your familiar physician takes the lead in managing your wellness and all other care needs—preventive, acute, chronic, and end-of-life.

Principle #4: coordinated and integrated care

When needs arise beyond the scope of primary care, the appropriate care is arranged with specialists, hospitals, home health agencies, and other healthcare and community services. The care received in the medical home is integrated appropriately with the care given from other providers to avoid unnecessary tests or treatments and to assure a smooth transition from one level of care to the other.

Principle #5: quality and safety

Although quality and safety are hallmarks of the medical home in every aspect of care, the use of information technology (with a focus on the Electronic Health Record) is vital to optimal patient care. The Electronic Health Record (EHR – which is also referred to as the Electronic Medical Record, EMR) is the best source for the kind of accurate, readable, and organized patient information, which helps your doctor make the best decisions about your care. This record also allows your doctor to share important information about you with any other providers who are involved in your care. We'll explain the value of the EHR and how it affects care quality and safety in more detail below.

Principal #6: enhanced access

The goal of this medical home principle is to assure that care is available through such measures as open scheduling (holding open a strategic number of time slots for same-day appointments), expanded hours (evenings and weekends), and more options for communication between you and your healthcare team, including a secure, online patient portal. Combined with the EHR, these online connections make it possible for patients to easily access test results, re-fill prescriptions, and email questions, among other transactions. In all cases, convenient access and timely communication are essential components of quality medical care, patient trust, and patient satisfaction.

Principal #7: payments

This component refers to a revised physician reimbursement structure that recognizes the added value that patients receive through a medical home. It's intended to make sure that physician and non-physician staff are fairly compensated for the significant amount of ongoing care management, communication, preventive services, education, and coordination efforts that fall outside the traditional billing codes of a face-to-face visit.

On the most basic level, payment reforms associated with the preventive care and early detection associated with a medical home create a comparatively small outlay of money with a monumental return on investment in terms of the total health system.

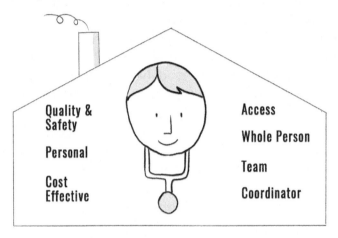

OUT WITH THE OLD, IN WITH THE NEW

You're probably familiar with the EHR as the program your doctor uses to record your information on the computer during an appointment. Long gone are the days when paper charts were sufficient to accurately record, organize, and keep current all of a patient's data points and history—especially the amount of detail needed for an older patient with several chronic conditions. The EHR is a great advancement for medical records and absolutely critical for competent, cost-effective care.

The EHR gives a complete picture of your medical history and condition, provides reminders to your doctor when it's time for routine tests, notifies him or her of your drug interactions, and helps keep your treatment plan on track. It also acts as an evaluation tool to measure your providers' quality of care through quantitative and qualitative data.

A well-functioning medical home depends on the EHR because it facilitates communication between all members of the care team and enhances coordination at every level. Every provider involved in your care outside your primary medical home can receive this same information and document each step to avoid unnecessary or even incorrect treatment. For communications spread even more widely, the interoperability of the EHR (multiple systems with potentially different formats exchanging information) removes redundancies and fragmentation among your extended healthcare team and prevents you from suffering the effects of poor care quality due to information that isn't accurately updated and shared. Note that the interoperability of some different EHR systems is not 100% in place yet, but significant progress has been made and continues.

WHAT THE MEDICAL HOME MEANS TO YOU

One of the most important lessons we've learned over decades of practicing medicine and advocating for the cause of primary care in the broader healthcare arena is that there's rarely, if ever, a single strategy for success, whether it's a clinical treatment or an advance in care delivery. But a strong basis of primary care— and increased use of the medical home that supports it—will effectively bring about the best elements of healthcare reform, including more convenient, affordable, and quality-driven care for you and your family. Your medical home will focus on prevention, chronic care management, and cost containment, shifting the emphasis of healthcare from disease treatment to health preservation and sustaining the vital relationship with your familiar physician.

The good news when it comes to finding a physician practice that operates as a medical home is that the numbers are growing rapidly nationwide. Information on being part of a public or private Patient-Centered Medical Home, many of which are recognized by the National Committee for Quality Assurance, an independent nationwide healthcare accreditation and organization, is available through a wide range of resources, including:

- U.S. Department of Health and Human Services

- State health departments
- Primary care physician organizations and associations
- The Patient-Centered Primary Care Collaborative
- Consumer-directed media, including *Consumer Reports*

It's worth doing a little research to find quality-driven, cost-saving care that's not only more satisfying to receive as a patient, but also more rewarding to provide as a clinician. The expectation is that the number of practices that have already adopted the medical home model and those in the process of transforming will continue to rapidly increase. Your health and the health of your family matter too much not to take advantage of this significant healthcare innovation as soon as possible.

Chapter 4:

ROBUST PRIMARY CARE: THE FOUNDATION OF AMERICAN HEALTHCARE

Some of our readers might remember the late comedian and actor Rodney Dangerfield, who became famous for reminding his audience, "I don't get no respect!" Dangerfield managed to build a long and lucrative career on the theme of being underappreciated, and there are times when his catchphrase would seem to apply to primary care medicine as well.

On a similar note, if you've worked a few different jobs in your life, you've likely experienced one that fell into the "overworked and underpaid" variety. You know what we're talking about: the job where you put in long hours, went above and beyond, and never got the recognition or compensation you deserved for all that exceptional effort.

Primary care physicians are all too familiar with this scenario. For example, despite their extensive post-medical school (residency) training, their broad and thorough knowledge base, and their direct impact on the lives of so many patients, primary care physicians (PCPs) face a considerable disparity in compensation—and often respect—with other doctors. In some cases, specialists generate three to four times more income than PCPs.

Physician training is another area where this disparity is evident. At least up until the last few years, medical schools like Johns Hopkins, Cornell, Harvard, Columbia, and Yale shared a reputation for producing some of the most highly trained physicians in the country. But none of them were prepared to be Family Medicine physicians, the discipline that makes up the majority of PCPs, because these and some of the other best medical programs in the U.S. didn't have, or still don't have, Family Medicine departments.

When you take into account that overworked and comparatively underpaid PCPs aren't expanding their ranks fast enough to replace the older doctors who are retiring from primary care (many of them burned out and leaving the field sooner than expected), it's no surprise that the PCP shortage is projected to continue well into the future. This scarcity would be a concern at any time. But now, with millions of newly-insured Americans, an aging population with many healthcare needs, and healthcare reform's focus on preventive care, population health management, and cost control (all of which primary care practices can handle well), the shortage of PCPs is even more critical.

Fortunately, the picture isn't entirely bleak. New medical schools and expanded admissions at existing ones are increasing the total number of doctors, although med students still have to choose residencies in primary care fields in order to become PCPs. In addition, the compensation gap between PCPs and specialist physicians is beginning to narrow for the first time in years. And the same emphasis that healthcare reform places on keeping people well instead of only treating them when they're sick also helps elevate primary care in terms of its place in the future of healthcare. Healthcare reform aims to strengthen the role of primary care through a number of structural changes, which include investment in the incentives and infrastructure needed to build a larger primary care workforce and new payment models that help refocus physicians on value instead of volume.

Business has also helped put primary care in the spotlight. IBM carried out a global study to determine if the two billion dollars the corporation spends each year on healthcare were being put to the best use. The consistent conclusion was that countries (such as Australia, the U.K., and the Netherlands) with the highest proportion of primary care also have the healthiest populations—and spend the lowest per capita on healthcare. An IBM study confined to the U.S. found that people with a regular source of primary care were more likely to comply with preventive care or treatment recommendations and experienced better outcomes at lower cost as a result.

All of these elements help reinforce the essential nature of a primary care-based delivery system as the foundation of effective and affordable healthcare—with PCPs serving as the pillars that rise to support everything built on top of it.

THE FOUR ESSENTIAL ATTRIBUTES OF ROBUST PRIMARY CARE

1. First Contact

Primary care is traditionally the first point of contact with the healthcare system when an illness or medical issue arises. While the primary care physician is the "go to" provider for health concerns, she or he is also a first-line resource for health promotion and maintenance, as well as disease prevention.

2. Comprehensive

Unlike specialists who direct their skills and training to a particular diagnosis, single organ, anatomical area, or a specific disease or technique, PCPs (sometimes referred to appropriately within the medical field as comprehensivists) specialize in treating the whole person. With that focus in mind, chronic care management for problems like diabetes, high blood pressure, arthritis, and heart disease are best handled by PCPs. At the same time, PCPs view every encounter with their patients as an opportunity for prevention or health education.

3. Continuous

The idea here is that the same physician cares for the same patient over time. Continuity

---

A QUICK GUIDE TO PRIMARY CARE PHYSICIANS

The Institute of Medicine, a division of the National Academies of Sciences, Engineering and Medicine, defines primary care as "The provision of integrated accessible healthcare services by clinicians who are accountable for addressing a large majority of personal healthcare needs, developing a sustained partnership with patients, and practicing in the context of family and community." The physician disciplines that follow are the principal providers of primary care in the United States:

- **Family Medicine Physicians:** treat patients of all ages and medical conditions
- **Pediatricians:** treat children from infants to 18 years of age
- **Internal Medicine Physicians (or Internists):** treat adults 18 years of age and older
- **Geriatric Medicine Physicians (typically trained in Internal Medicine):** treat elderly adults

is an absolute necessity for a mutually trusting, respectful, and strong patient-physician bond. A great deal of research indicates that people who have an established relationship with their PCP experience better outcomes and less costly care.

4. Coordination

Because of his or her role as a patient's advocate who manages care throughout the total healthcare system, the PCP has been called the "captain of the ship," "general contractor," and "conductor of the symphony." While these analogies offer some sense of what the PCP does, the actual coordinating function involves a skillful and seamless connectivity with appropriate resources as necessary—including specialists, tests, hospitalization, and community services—for optimal patient health as well as cost effectiveness.

IMPORTANT THINGS TO KNOW

As Bob Dylan famously sang, you don't need a weatherman to know which way the wind blows. Similarly, you don't have to be a healthcare policy analyst, a physician, or a hospital administrator to see how primary care-based healthcare is positioned to increase long-term quality of care and decrease costs when compared to our current specialist-based delivery system.

Regardless of how you look at the data, it simply makes sense that preventing problems before they become more serious is the way to go. In the case of healthcare, it's better for total population health, and it's better for the national economy.

But while this big picture of healthcare has relevance for all of us, we have to be realistic about what we, personally, can do on such a large stage. Since the ballot box hasn't figured all that prominently in the current state of healthcare (and assuming you're not planning on getting elected to Congress), you have a rather limited ability to influence challenges such as funding and policy as a means to invigorate the primary care infrastructure. But here's what you can do on a very personal level:

EVEN MORE IMPORTANT THINGS TO DO

The Centers for Disease Control and Prevention estimate that only about 55% of healthcare encounters are happening within the primary care sector. The rest are taking place in emergency rooms and urgent care centers—a far more costly primary care substitute—or directly within specialist disciplines. The millions of Americans who lack access to primary care come from all income levels, racial backgrounds, and ethnic groups. Many of them have some level of health coverage, but beyond access limited by geography or the PCP shortage, what they lack is a high-functioning medical home led by their familiar physician.

If physician scarcity or costs aren't issues standing in your way, the first step is to find and get to know a familiar physician. If you already have a doctor who doesn't seem to exhibit the four essential attributes of primary care we mentioned, isn't particularly responsive, or talks a lot without listening, consider switching to a different provider. Sometimes it just comes down to preference in terms of personality and professional style. Like any relationship, the one between you and your familiar physician has to work well for both parties.

An extensive survey conducted by *Consumer Reports* found that a recommendation from a person's family, friends, or coworkers was still the preferred way to find and choose a new PCP, followed by referrals from other doctors or related healthcare providers. There are a number of online "report cards" in most locations, too, as well as a website developed by the Centers for Medicare and Medicaid Services (CMS) called Physician Compare. At the time of this writing, Physician Compare is set up to help find and choose only those doctors who accept Medicare patients, but the service is expected to expand.

Once you have a familiar physician, the next important issue is to make sure his or her practice is moving toward incorporating the characteristics of a medical home. Currently there are a relatively small but quickly growing number of recognized Patient-Centered Medical Home practices. Even if your familiar physician isn't part of an "official" medical home, however, you'll want a relationship with a doctor who supports its easy-access concept and teamwork structure and is committed to running a patient-centered practice through staffing, clinical approach, and personal philosophy.

THE BOTTOM LINE

There's one sure way to determine if you and the whole approach to health represented by familiar physicians, medical homes, and primary care are a good fit. For a moment, put aside the details about the benefits of team care, accessibility, continuity, coordination, and lower costs, and just ask yourself a few basic questions:

- *Do you want to spend more years around friends and loved ones?*
- *Do you want to participate in the things you enjoy with more vitality and a greater sense of well-being?*
- *Do you want to avoid unnecessary tests, surgeries, and hospitalizations?*
- *Do you want to experience better overall health and quality of life?*

If you answered "yes" to any of these questions (and who wouldn't?), it's time to start partnering with your familiar physician to make those goals a reality.

Chapter 5:

THERE'S A NEW TEAM IN THE EXAM ROOM (AND YOU NEED TO BE ON IT)

IN *THE BOYS IN the Boat*, a masterful account of the University of Washington's eight-oar crew in the 1936 Olympics in Berlin, author Daniel James Brown offers insight into what it takes to develop a gold medal-winning team. He also describes the frustration of the university's rowing coach as he kept trying to put together the best combination of people, a task he finally realized relied on temperament, personality, and other intangibles as much as it did on physical strength and rowing skills.

Each time he assigned nine young men to a racing shell—eight rowers and a coxswain—he was fulfilling the basic requirement of building a team. But only when he found people who shared common goals, and then sublimated some, but not all, of their personal interests toward those goals, did he engage in true team building. Simply put, he learned that building a team was an action, while team building was a concept and a vision.

As you've probably already guessed, we think there's a strong analogy between a well-rowed racing boat and a team approach to primary care medicine. And while physician practices include multiple functions and physical spaces that impact your health, all of which benefit from closer cooperation between staff, the team approach to care is most important in the exam room. That's the place where the relationship between you and your doctor is formed and strengthened and where a surprisingly simple change in primary care delivery is poised to make a critical difference in the quality of the care you receive.

But we've gotten just a little bit ahead of ourselves. Before looking at how this innovation takes place, let's look first at why exam room innovation is so desperately needed.

WELCOME TO THE EXAM ROOM MUSEUM

If a physician practicing in 1930 or even earlier could have been transported into the future to arrive at a present-day medical exam room, he (there's very little chance it would have been a she back then) would, with few exceptions, look around at the surroundings without expressing much surprise. He'd observe some updated equipment and technology to be sure, including the computer-based Electronic Health Record (EHR), but for the most part would be spared of any major future shock.

In terms of process, however, the differences would be even less noticeable. The physician-centric approach to the exam room that has universally prevailed in America for almost 100 years is part of a tradition that stretches back over even more centuries. The traditional exam room activity consists of a doctor performing virtually all the clinical and clerical work required for the visit. Since modern medicine began phasing out the house call in the 1920s, we've accepted the idea that only the doctor belongs in the exam room, despite the fact that today at least 60% of the work carried out there doesn't require the expertise of a physician. The time-consuming process of EHR data entry has accentuated this ineffectiveness and misuse of a doctor's skill. Unlike the change dynamic and innovation that seems to be built into other industries and the ongoing evolution of process-related tools and resources, apparently no one did a workflow analysis on the exam room.

That's where healthcare is at a disadvantage. Few if any other fields of endeavor could sustain this lack of process innovation in general with its overly centralized approach to work distribution in particular. Primary care medicine, however, has managed to limp along and continues to do so in many practices where non-physician tasks are still handled by a medical doctor, contributing to backups in the waiting room and a sub-par experience in the exam room. This scenario isn't doing the physician any good either, as it often results in longer days and more work taken home.

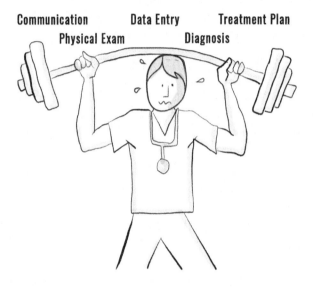

While the current exam room process might not cause much of a stir for our hypothetical time-traveling physician, other changes swirling around primary care would definitely be noticed. The most notable include an increased number of aging adults with chronic diseases, an explosion of growth in the pharmaceutical industry, a rise in malpractice concerns, an expanded regulatory environment, a growing pool of recently insured patients, and the integration of the EHR. In fact, just about everything has changed except the exam room delivery process.

Fortunately, there's a better inside-the-exam-room approach now being used by a growing number of practices that relies on sharing responsibilities while enabling the doctor to focus on what she or he is singularly trained to do—not unlike the well-established team dynamic found in the operating room.

PRIMARY CARE: IT TAKES A TEAM

The team approach in the exam room begins with the idea that healthcare professionals can and should work at the top of their licensure or regulated scope of practice. What that means in a practical sense is that other clinical staff should be mobilized to practice their skills to the full extent of their training and education. As a result, physicians can share tasks with other staff members who perform at what's generally a lower cost.

In the primary care exam room, it begins with a specially trained medical assistant or nurse who opens your visit by asking you symptom or disease-associated questions (based on physician-developed protocols) for your current episode of care. He or she enters your information into the EHR and updates your records as needed. When your doctor enters the room, the clinical assistant verbally presents your data for verification (on the part of the patient) and completion. The assistant documents the rest of the visit, reinforces the treatment plan, and provides follow-up information.

The result is a win on every level. The physician is freed up to direct his or her full attention to you with regard to diagnosis and treatment, as well as any required coordination with specialists or other care providers. You're able to maintain a direct and uninterrupted conversation with the physician during your appointment. The two of you gain a stronger relationship and a more enduring bond of trust, which research shows is associated with improved patient outcomes. At the same time the clinical staff, with their increased training and empowerment, enjoy a greater sense of workplace satisfaction. And looking at the larger picture, the care delivery itself is more efficient, effective, and less costly.

TAKE YOUR PLACE ON THE CARE TEAM

One of the other positive changes that have occurred while the exam room process languished in the past is a much stronger focus on involving you, the patient, in the process itself. This greater participation is associated with a more informed consumer, but also with what seems to be a sincere effort on the part of physician practices, hospitals, and other healthcare entities to create a more collaborative experience.

Open any website for a physician practice, hospital, or clinic, and you're bound to see multiple references to "patient-centered care," "patient-driven care," "healthcare centered around you," or some other promise that you're going to be part of the decision-making process and take a more active role in your own care. The promise also includes discussing options with your doctor and gathering information about costs—concepts that were virtually unheard of in medicine not so very long ago. Are these healthcare providers really committed to bring you on board as a fully functioning member of the multidisciplinary teams we've been discussing? Assume they are and act accordingly. As primary care medicine moves from a traditional medical practice model to team-based care, it's essential that you get on the team.

AND TALK BACK TO YOUR HEALTHCARE PROVIDER

Back in 1970 a former member of the Federal Communications Commission published a book, *How to Talk Back to Your*

Television Set. The issue he focused on was the passive acceptance of information and the lack of interactivity with what had become a dominant force in our society. New technology and a tsunami of social media have rendered the limitations of television obsolete—though not yet the medium itself. But what's still relevant is the concern, and now we're talking about healthcare again, of passively receiving information and accepting advice without respectfully discussing those recommendations, asking appropriate questions, or expressing your thoughts and feelings.

Ultimately, a more collaborative and convenient approach to healthcare isn't something you should simply hope for; it's something you should expect. If you find that the next time you're in an exam room with a doctor and she or he is eyeballing a computer screen instead of you, ask why another team member can't be involved in the data entry and documentation part of your visit. If the physician's office tells you to head for the urgent care center because it's after normal hours, ask what's keeping them for expanding their schedule. If your shared costs of care represent a hardship for you and your family, don't hesitate to talk about alternatives.

And whatever you do, don't give up on American healthcare, despite its current state of flux. After dragging its feet for decades behind banking, travel, hospitality, and a wide range of service industries, healthcare is beginning to enter the Age of the Consumer. Health systems and individual physicians are improving everything from staff training to communications infrastructure in order to deliver an improved customer experience. It's not quite here yet, at least in a consistent way, but it's definitely coming.

Chapter 6:

AT THE INTERSECTION OF MONEY AND MEDICINE

AS ACTOR AND COMEDIAN Chris Rock said, "Wealth isn't about having a lot of money; it's about having a lot of options." Yet in the case of healthcare, we generally end up with very few options in relation to the amount of personal and national wealth we expend. And the repercussions of costly healthcare affect our other options as well.

We talked a bit about the problem earlier, but the concern is worth repeating: the financial issues facing healthcare have created a crisis that's impacting our economic security. While there have been a few rare times when the rates of cost increase were more modest, including the 2007 to 2009 recession, healthcare spending has consistently exceeded—far exceeded—wage growth in the United States, as well as the national economy itself. The result is an overwhelming burden on the government as well as on businesses and individuals.

Although the government forecasts that the high rates of healthcare spending will continue at least through 2024, there are some changes on the horizon that can help provide more control for our nation's expanding health tab while simultaneously improving healthcare quality. The Accountable Care Organization (ACO) stands out among those changes.

THE ABCS OF HEALTHCARE ARE FOCUSING ON ACOS

If you were of a certain age in the 1980s, you probably remember the introduction of a new alphabet soup of terms— like HMOs, PPOs, PMPM, MCOs, POS, and a host of others— associated with managed care. Managed care is a contractual agreement between insurance companies and healthcare systems designed to improve quality and lower costs. Some of the elements of managed care have ended up on the proverbial trash heap of history, but others continue today.

If managed care's goals of increased quality and decreased costs sound familiar, it's because virtually all efforts at healthcare reform hope to bring together those two attributes, with better access to care forming the third leg of the stool. The Accountable Care Organization is no exception. We'll look at how ACOs are different when compared to the first generation of managed care, but first let's talk briefly about what ACOs are.

SHARING THE RISKS AND REWARDS

An ACO is a network of healthcare providers such as physicians, hospitals, ambulatory surgery centers, home health agencies, pharmacies, and other services that voluntarily come together to take on a shared responsibility for delivering care to a specific group of patients. These patients are known in the medical world as a "population." In all cases, the ACO must have a strong base of primary care practices. As a collective group of healthcare providers, the ACO participants work together to plan budgets, determine resource needs, and put reliable performance measures in place.

In addition to their joint accountability for quality, cost, and overall health of their population, the members of an ACO also share in the savings that result from reducing costs. This means ACOs can generate a profit for the network and its individual participants when, on the most basic level, they provide good care and control costs.

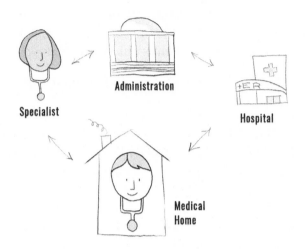

Specialist

Administration

Hospital

Medical
Home

In case you're wondering if costs in an ACO are decreased through rationing services or denying or delaying care—one of those third-rail political issues that rightfully concern a lot of people and the elected officials who represent them—you can breathe easy. ACOs help control the cost of healthcare through a number of opportunities that *don't* place restrictions on care, including improved prevention and early diagnosis, reductions in preventable emergency room visits and readmissions to hospitals, improved efficiencies across the board, and the reduction of adverse events (anything that causes unintentional harm to a patient as a result of a medical intervention).

A SHORT HISTORY OF ACOS

The ACO as it exists today is a product of the Affordable Care Act (ACA). Specifically, Title III of the ACA includes a provision called "Encouraging Development of New Patient Care Models." It's worth noting that the ACO is one of the least politicized provisions in the ACA and one of the very few that's maintained fairly strong bipartisan support for its efforts to add value and accountability to the healthcare system and to the people it serves.

As originally defined through the ACA, ACOs were directed only to Medicare beneficiaries. Now they're available through private insurers so people of all ages can take advantage of the improved coordination they offer. These commercial ACOs are similar to the Medicare model, but the private sector insurers determine their own measurements for quality and feature some contractual differences from one insurer to another. Both the number of Medicare and commercial ACOs has grown considerably since their initial implementation and now includes millions of patients across the country. It's reasonable to expect that within the next couple of years, a high percentage of the money that comes into the healthcare system will be routed through ACOs.

AND AN EVEN SHORTER COMPARISON OF ACOS AND HMOS

As mentioned, the managed care organizations that emerged in the 1980s (of which Health Maintenance Organizations [HMOs] were the most publicized model) and today's ACOs share some common goals with regard to care integration and lower costs. But there are three important differences that make the ACO a better option. First, while healthcare consumers had to join HMOs, it's the care providers who join and form the ACO. Second, unlike the more flexible and patient-friendly ACO, HMOs have certain operational features that limit patient choices, including referrals to specialists. Third and maybe most important of all, an ACO patient is not required to stay within the network—the care providers who are part of a particular plan or group—in order to receive care, possibly without incurring additional costs.

BUNDLE UP: A BETTER WAY TO PAY FOR HEALTHCARE

When the initial ACOs were set up for Medicare as part of the Accountable Care Act, they all used the traditional fee-for-service (FFS) method of paying healthcare providers. In the FFS form of compensation, physicians are paid for each procedure they perform, regardless of whether or not it proves to be beneficial to the patient. Because every test, every visit, every service is billed separately, there's a built-in incentive to maximize the number of procedures done, putting the emphasis on quantity instead of quality. This kind of system contributes to the blank check our society has handed healthcare, an approach that always creates extravagance. And it favors specialists who perform the most complex and expensive procedures, while marginalizing primary care doctors who spend more time interacting with patients and delivering comparatively routine, lower-cost services.

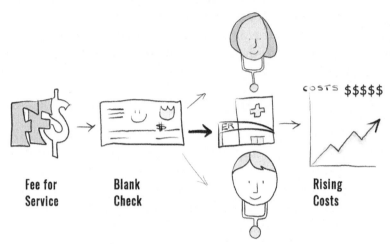

Fee for Service   **Blank Check**   **Rising Costs**

Specialist/Hospital/Primary Care

Changing this current financial structure is a critical step in reaching the kind of prevention-based, patient-centered care that is envisioned for healthcare reform. Toward that objective, in the spring of 2015 U.S. Health and Human Services Secretary Silvia M. Burwell announced a timeline to move the Medicare program toward paying providers based on the value they provide (measured as a combination of improved outcomes and reduced costs), not the sheer volume of procedures they carry out. Because Medicare is one of the largest health insurance programs in the world, its impact on the rest of U.S. healthcare is significant. This change in the way medicine is paid for will continue to positively impact our entire health system.

This transition from a compensation system based on volume to one that promotes value includes what is referred to as "bundled" payments. As you might imagine from the name, bundled payments combine the costs of the various medical encounters that a patient experiences into a single, pre-determined amount or lump sum based on total expected costs for a defined episode of care. By its nature, this type of payment model encourages increased coordination between the different participants in an ACO and makes everyone involved more attentive to the total costs of treating a patient. At the same time, bundled payments reward those providers who keep their patients healthier. This model of payment also places greater value on the non-procedural but highly important aspects of care like a stronger patient-physician bond and more involvement in decision making on the part of the patient and family.

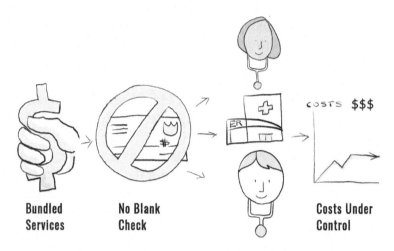

| Bundled Services | No Blank Check | | Costs Under Control |

Specialist/Hospital/Primary Care

WHAT IT MEANS FOR HEALTHCARE AND YOUR CARE

Getting relief from healthcare costs that reduce U.S. competitiveness in international markets and divert funds needed for other programs and initiatives is a national priority. But even as we realize healthcare is consuming a larger and larger part of our total economy, the negative impact on something as abstract as our Gross Domestic Product doesn't directly translate into something that has much meaning to you. And it should, because if there's a financial system for healthcare, there's a good chance that system is propped up with your money through federal and state tax dollars. On the employment-based health coverage front, increased healthcare costs are negating the growth of personal income through rapidly rising premiums and out-of-pocket costs. Employers who are paying more to provide health coverage may also delay wage increases. So beyond the national and even international impact of overly expensive healthcare, the problem hits close to home, too.

When they work up to their potential, ACOs represent a way to control costs without sacrificing the quality of care. Like virtually everything else in medicine, ACOs are not a panacea for what ails healthcare, but they're an absolutely needed step (and a large one at that) in the right direction. In the world of national healthcare, ACOs are an excellent vehicle for the Patient-Centered Medical Home we talked about earlier. Because of their emphasis on prevention and the kind of follow-up that provides improved management of chronic conditions, ACOs are also an important driver of making primary care the foundation of our health system. With a true primary care base and more reliance on outpatient rather than inpatient care, healthcare costs will go down significantly.

In your world, the results can be equally dramatic. The ACO focus on proactive care and the greater degree of coordination among all providers who are involved with your health holds the promise of improving quality of care. As we said, however, there's no perfect solution when it comes to creating better value and improved patient outcomes while spending healthcare dollars more wisely. And while cautious optimism is certainly in order, there are factions in healthcare for whom the jury is still out when it comes to ACOs. But in the alphabet soup of healthcare acronyms and abbreviations, there's a good chance that A-C-O spells the future.

Chapter 7:

EVERYTHING YOU *NEVER* WANTED TO KNOW ABOUT HEALTH INSURANCE BUT NEED TO

YOU MAY HAVE SEEN the Saturday Night Live "Old Glory Insurance" sketch some years back. In a parody of classic insurance commercials, a group of seniors sits around a coffee table discussing the perils of modern life, including gangs, rap music, and the increasing number of robots. But thanks to one couple's newly acquired Old Glory Insurance, they finally have a policy designed to protect the elderly from terrifying robot attacks.

While insurance can give you a measure of security from various threats (killer robots included for those with Old Glory), few people enjoy talking about it. Health coverage is no exception. At best it ranks near the bottom of things you want to deal with on any given day. At worst it's confusing, frustrating, and overly complex. But the fact is that health insurance, for the millions of Americans fortunate enough to have some level of coverage, is the best protection available against the potentially overwhelming costs of healthcare.

WHY MOST PEOPLE HAVEN'T PAID ATTENTION TO THE COST OF COVERAGE

Note: As a quick reference point, about one out of every three Americans is covered by Medicare or Medicaid. (See pages 67-69.) Beyond this large number (approximately 100 million people in both programs), the majority of Americans receive health coverage through their employer.

According to the Employee Benefit Research Institute, a nonpartisan, nonprofit research firm based in Washington, D.C., employment-based health coverage reached its peak in the late 1980s. Since that time it's been declining, and estimates are that within a decade or so, a high percentage of the American workers who now receive health insurance through their employers will transition into the government-administered health exchanges that have been created by the Affordable Care Act. More on that later, but in the meantime what we'll initially be talking about below is primarily related to employee-based coverage.

The simple answer to the question of why we don't pay much attention to health insurance is that many people haven't had to, despite the fact that healthcare costs have risen sharply over the past 30 years. Basically, if you have coverage, you've been sheltered from the reality of these increases because of the way employer-based insurance was structured.

For example, your insurance carrier might get a $400,000 bill for your hospital stay. You, on the other hand, probably wouldn't even be aware of this number unless you were uninsured or your insurance plan had a cap or limit. When you went to the doctor or hospital and got expensive tests, your insurance covered just about everything. Typically the only place you saw a cost increase was in the cost of the insurance itself, not in the expense of the actual healthcare services that were provided.

PAST

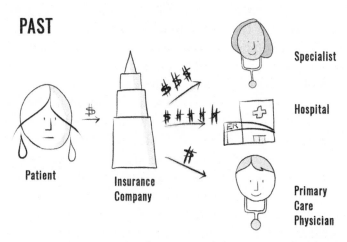

In this new era of healthcare reform, a significant portion of the expense of covered benefits is now shifting to you, and you're experiencing unfamiliar and unexpected financial responsibility. "Covered by insurance" really means insurance will cover much of the cost *after* high deductibles, copayments, and coinsurance. Along with being sheltered from costs, you were also sheltered from complexity. Commonly, you'd pay little attention to your employer's yearly insurance policy selection, grateful that someone else was evaluating and providing options so you didn't have to spend much time studying such a complicated matrix of information. Now, it's very likely that you're going to have to take more ownership of how the process works and how it affects you.

PRESENT

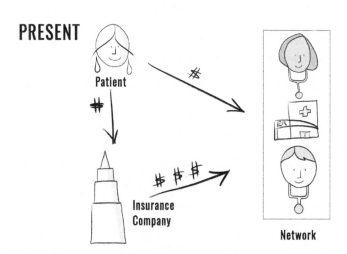

One notable change ushered in by the Affordable Care Act is the new Health Insurance Marketplace (also known as the "exchange"). If you don't have coverage and have a low income, this is where you can find an insurance plan that fits your needs and budget through federal subsidies and cost sharing.

The limited connection with direct payment for healthcare that many Americans have had up until this point also means that you may not have had to think much about the financial implications of choosing certain services or providers because insurance would handle the lion's share of the bill. Now that you're responsible to pay a greater percentage of costs out of pocket, and since huge variances exist in billing practices from provider to provider, you have to start thinking about (and even asking about) prices up front. You'd never buy a car without knowing how much it costs. The same should be true for healthcare.

These structural changes in our healthcare system should have a cost-cutting benefit in the long run because consumers will become more aware of actual costs now that they have a considerable share in the payment. It might not seem like it yet, but in reality, healthcare reform has standardized insurance to significantly simplify comparisons between options. Our new insurance world is still complex (and can be downright challenging at times), but hopefully this chapter will equip you with a clearer understanding of how to find your way through it and make better-informed choices.

A FEW DEFINITIONS

Before we dive in, here are some definitions of important terms and areas of cost you need to understand:

Acute care: immediate medical need requiring short-term treatment.

Allowed amount: the maximum amount (also called "eligible expense," "negotiated rate," and "payment allowance") your insurance plan will cover for a specific healthcare service. You may have to pay the difference if you see a provider who charges more than the allowed amount. (See "balance billing.")

Balance billing: when an out-of-network provider bills you for the remaining balance after your insurance pays its allowed amount for non-network providers. You won't encounter balance billing with a preferred (in-network) provider because he or she provides services as part of the insurance network agreement.

Benefits: healthcare services that are covered under your insurance plan.

Chronic care management: routine follow-up to manage long-term illness.

Coinsurance: your share of the costs for a specific covered service. This amount is calculated as a percentage (e.g., 30%) of the amount your plan allows for the service. You pay the coinsurance amount and any deductible you owe, and your plan covers the rest of the allowed amount for the service.

Copayment: fixed amount (e.g., $20, $30, $50) you pay when you receive services covered by your health plan (usually paid at the time services are rendered). The copay amount varies by your plan and the type of service you receive.

Cost sharing: the share of costs for benefits that you pay out-of-pocket. This generally includes deductibles, coinsurance, copayments, or similar charges but doesn't include premiums, the cost of non-covered services, or balance billing for non-network providers. Individuals with low income who are buying insurance plans from the Health Insurance Marketplace may qualify for cost-sharing financial assistance.

Deductible: the amount you pay out-of-pocket for covered services before your insurance pays the balance.

Diagnostic care: intervention sought for symptoms or complications of an illness. These tests are necessary for managing illness and not considered preventive care, so coinsurance rules apply (in contrast to preventive tests which are free).

Out-of-pocket costs: your expenses for health services that aren't reimbursed by your insurance plan. These include deductibles, copayments, and coinsurance for covered services and the costs of all non-covered services.

Out-of-pocket maximum/limit: the most you'll have to pay during a policy year before your plan starts to cover 100% of the costs for essential benefits (listed on pages 60-61). This amount includes deductibles, coinsurance, copayments, or any other costs for medically necessary care covered by your plan. It doesn't include premiums, out-of-network costs, or the costs of non-covered services. Once you reach your plan's maximum, you won't have any more out-of-pocket expenses for the rest of the policy year. (2015 plans purchased on the Marketplace have a $6,600 maximum per individual and $13,200 per family. This amount can seem high, but it gives you the security of an established ceiling—you won't face a $50,000 or $100,000 bill.)

Premium: the annual amount you pay for your insurance plan's covered benefits (usually paid in monthly installments). The higher the monthly payments, the lower the out-of-pocket costs for services received during the year.

Preventive care/services: routine care (when you're symptom-free) such as physical exams, recommended screenings, and patient education/counseling to prevent illness or disease. This care is fully covered by insurance as long as the insurance was obtained after the ACA went into effect. (See "Grandfathered Health Plans" on page 82.) Visit healthcare.gov/preventive-care-benefits to see a full list of preventive services available at no cost to you.

We'll explain other terms as we encounter them in this chapter. (You can also visit the Glossary of Terms in the Appendix to find other definitions or to refresh your memory.)

ESSENTIAL BENEFITS COVERED BY ALL INSURANCE PLANS

While there are certain exemptions, the Affordable Care Act (ACA) essentially requires everyone to have health insurance. It also mandates that all of the insurance plans you can sign up for during the Open Enrollment period (more on this on page 76) must provide at least the following 10 essential benefits. Some plans will offer other benefits in addition to these:

1. Outpatient care, acute care, and chronic care management (provided in practices and clinics)
2. Emergency Room care
3. Care if you are admitted to a hospital and/or require surgery
4. Pre- and post-natal care
5. Mental health and substance use disorder services (includes counseling and psychotherapy)
6. Medications (though coverage may be limited)
7. Rehabilitative services and devices to assist with injuries, disabilities, and chronic conditions
8. Lab tests, X-rays, and other tests deemed medically necessary
9. Preventive care
10. Dental and vision care for children (not adults)

The ACA also designates several additional boundaries to standardize insurance plans. For example, no person may be denied health insurance no matter how many pre-existing health issues he or she has. There are no limitations placed on the consumer for how much insurance will pay for his or her particular healthcare needs.

Additionally, there are no price increases for insurance coverage due to pre-existing conditions. The only price increases or differences are related to age (older adults can be charged up to three times more for premiums), group (insurers can charge more for a plan that covers family members), geographic location (cost of living—including healthcare—varies based on where you live), tobacco use, and the specific health plan. (See pages 176-179 in the appendix for more details on essential benefits.)

HOW TO PICK AN INSURANCE PLAN

Step 1: Start with your physician. If you have an existing primary care physician, find out the insurance plans in which she or he participates.

Step 2: Find the right place for you to buy your insurance plan. You can obtain your insurance through your employer, the Health Insurance Marketplace, private insurance companies, Medicaid and Medicare (for those older than 65 or eligible for free or low-cost healthcare), or from an insurance agent/broker.

Step 3: Select your level of cost sharing. This level is determined by the ACA-designated "Metal Plans"—Bronze, Silver, Gold, and Platinum—to represent the cost structure. (See pages 71-72.) Keep in mind that actual costs may vary. In other words, one company's Silver plan may cost more than another's Gold plan. There's also a Catastrophic plan that is generally limited to adults 30 years old or younger.

The actual percentage you pay depends on which cost-sharing level you choose. The level you choose determines how you share costs with your insurance but doesn't affect the quality or amount of care you receive.

Step 4: Select a network and the set of rules that govern that network. A network represents the group of providers, facilities, and suppliers your insurance company has contracted with to provide the healthcare services you may need. The rules govern how you get care inside and outside this network. This contractual agreement between an insurance company and network with a set of rules constitutes managed care.

Step 5: Select the appropriate insurance plan. This is the plan that has your doctor in its network, has acceptable network rules, and fits your financial situation.

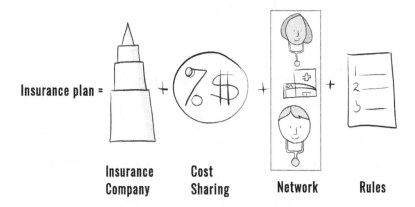

Insurance plan =

Insurance   Cost
Company   Sharing   Network   Rules

DETAILED STEPS FOR INSURANCE PLAN SELECTION

Step 1: Start with your physician

We've already shared with you the value of having a long-term familiar physician. The selection of your primary care doctor is the most important healthcare decision you'll make. This choice affects how you spend your healthcare dollars and can help shape your health for the rest of your life.

Many people choose a physician based on their insurance plan. They pick their insurance first, they find out which doctors are in the network, and then they select a doctor from that group of providers. The problem with that approach is if you initially choose a provider who proves not to be a good fit (or if you don't have primary care physician at all), you can find yourself in a difficult and expensive situation when you need care.

For that reason, it's a good idea to select a doctor first and your insurance plan second. In other words, choose a good doctor based on the kinds of criteria we described earlier and then find out the insurance program in which she or he participates. In some cases the health plan may be a little more expensive, but the comfort as well as the direct health benefits of having a strong professional relationship with your PCP are worth the difference.

Step 2: Find the right place for you to buy your insurance plan

You can find and enroll in a health plan several different ways:

Employer-Sponsored Health Plan

If you have an employer-sponsored health plan, this is almost always the best place for you to choose your insurance. You may not be able to pick the doctor you want right away due to a limited primary care panel (the physicians who participate in the plan). But panels change and doctors shift plan participation, so you should keep your eye on his or her availability in your plan. Be watchful and choose early in the selection cycle, as many primary care practices fill up quickly.

Employers have an interest in helping their employees to become better healthcare shoppers. Higher deductibles represent one way to ensure employees understand the cost impact of their healthcare decisions. A plan with a high deductible will have less expensive monthly payments. But then you'll pay more when you actually need care.

Employers' plans may also limit the allowed amount for certain diagnostic or treatment procedures. Relatively common procedures such as a knee replacement can generally be obtained at reasonable prices. But some specialists charge significantly more than others for the exact same procedure, which means you'd pay the difference between the plan allowance and the actual cost of the procedure—a potentially high price. Make sure you know what your plan's allowed amounts are and research costs before getting a procedure.

Again, if you aren't limited by the insurance plans offered through your employer, pick your doctor first, double check the availability for new patients if you're new to that doctor, and then choose one of the insurance plans that the practice accepts.

Health Insurance Marketplace

The Health Insurance Marketplace (also called the "exchange") helps those who don't have insurance find and enroll in a plan. If you don't have coverage through a job, Medicare, Medicaid, the Children's Health Insurance Program (CHIP),

VA medical care for military service veterans, or elsewhere, the Marketplace is where you can go to select a plan that meets your needs and fits your budget. All Marketplace plans cover essential health benefits (listed on pages 60-61), preventive care, and pre-existing conditions.

Applicants for Marketplace plans may qualify for savings on deductibles, copayments, and other costs (known as cost sharing). Applicants with limited income, disabilities, or other special circumstances may also qualify for Medicaid or CHIP. In addition, households that meet certain income requirements and don't have access to affordable health insurance through an employer or another government program may qualify to receive federal subsidies.

Eligibility for certain government programs and benefits, including federal subsidies and cost sharing related to health coverage available through the Health Insurance Marketplace, is based on a standard called the Federal Poverty Level (FPL). The FPL is a measure of income issued annually by the Department of Health and Human Services. The parameters change based on the current cost of living. Plans obtained through the Marketplace are the only way to access the FPL-related subsidies and cost sharing. (Note that this brief discussion of FPL may require you to put your math hat on for a short time, but if you meet the eligibility requirements and you're looking to save on coverage, this is valuable information and worth working through the numbers and percentages.)

If your annual income falls between 133-400% of the FPL, you can qualify for a federal subsidy to help buy coverage. If your income falls below 250% of the FPL, you may also be eligible for cost sharing. The federal subsidy caps the cost of health insurance between 2% and 9.5% of annual household income, depending on how much money is made relative to the FPL. (To give you some reference points, 400% of the FPL for an individual will be $47,080 and $97,000 for a family of four in 2016. The parameters are higher in Alaska and Hawaii, where the cost of living is higher.)

Medicaid covers those living 100% below the FPL, but a gap exists between Medicaid and federal subsidy eligibility for states that haven't expanded Medicaid to cover those living between

100-133% of the FPL. Federally Qualified Health Centers (FQHCs) help serve this population gap. (See pages 81, 98.)

When it comes to purchasing insurance through the Marketplace, it's important to understand where you fall on the FPL so you can determine whether or not you're eligible for Medicaid in your state, a federal subsidy because you earn between 133-400% of the FPL, or a subsidy because you purchased a Silver plan and earn less than 250% of the FPL.

If you qualify for a subsidy, the amount can be deducted 100% (or less) from the monthly premiums, or it can be deferred to the end of the year. Most people choose to have the maximum deducted monthly. (Note that these money-related transactions have potential impact on federal taxes.)

Any consumer can shop both on and off the Marketplace, and health plan areas of cost (premiums, deductibles, coinsurance, copayments, out-of-pocket maximums) are essentially the same either way. But as mentioned before, the Marketplace is the only place to get tax subsidies and cost sharing to help cover the monthly premium and out-of-pocket expenses.

You can apply for a Marketplace plan online, by phone, or with a paper application. Visit healthcare.gov/quick-guide for more information.

You can also view a chart to help you assess your eligibility for lower costs on coverage (based on income/household size and your state's Medicaid expansion) at healthcare.gov/lower-costs.

Social Services

Medicaid

When you fill out a Marketplace application, you may discover that you're eligible for coverage through Medicaid or the Children's Health Insurance Program (CHIP). Both of these are jointly run federal and state programs that provide free or low-cost health coverage to low-income families, children, and individuals. Medicaid beneficiaries can also include pregnant women, the elderly, individuals with disabilities, parents/ caretaker relatives, and other non-disabled, non-elderly adults. Eligibility is based on factors such as income, age, disability, or household size.

CHIP and Medicaid work closely together within each state,

and coverage provided by these programs varies from state to state. Medicaid coverage is currently expanding in many states to include all households below certain income levels.

If you have health coverage through Medicaid or CHIP, you meet the coverage requirements of healthcare law. You don't have to buy a Marketplace plan or pay the tax penalty for not having health coverage. (See "Uninsured Tax Penalty" on page 78.)

For complete Medicaid information, visit medicaid.gov.

Medicare

Medicare is a federal health insurance program for those age 65 and older. It also provides coverage for certain people with disabilities who are younger than 65. If you're age 65 or older, you can enroll through Social Security and access everything online. You should sign up for Medicare three months before reaching age 65, even if you plan to delay receiving retirement benefits because you will continue working. Medicare's four parts—Part A, Part B, Part C, and Part D—cover different types of healthcare services:

Original Medicare (Part A and Part B): Most Medicare beneficiaries have coverage through Original Medicare, which includes Part A and Part B and is administered by the government through Medicare Administrative Contractors (MACs). Part A is considered hospital insurance and covers most hospital, nursing facility, home health, and hospice care. This coverage is free if you've worked and paid Social Security taxes for 10 years or more. If you've worked and paid taxes for less than 10 years, you'll pay a monthly premium for coverage. Part B is Medical Insurance, which covers most preventive care, provider services, medical equipment, hospital outpatient care, lab tests, X-rays, mental health services, and some home health and ambulance services. You pay a monthly premium for Part B coverage.

Medicare Advantage Plan (Part C): You can also choose to enroll in a Medicare Advantage plan, also called Medicare Part C, which is offered by private insurance companies that contract with Medicare. Part C isn't a separate benefit; it's a private health plan that provides you with Medicare coverage as an alternative to Original Medicare. Part C plans are required to provide at least the same benefits as Part A and Part B of Original Medicare but operate with different rules, costs, and restrictions. There are many Advantage plan options available. Some provide prescription drug coverage, or you can choose Part D as part of the benefits package included in your plan. You may pay a monthly premium for Advantage plan coverage.

Part D: Medicare Part D is Outpatient Prescription Drug Insurance, which provides your outpatient prescription drug coverage. This part of Medicare is provided through private insurance companies engaged in contracts with the federal government. If you have Original Medicare (Part A and Part B), you should choose a stand-alone Part D plan.

Medicare Supplement Insurance: Medicare beneficiaries may also obtain a separate policy that covers the gaps in coverage of Medicare. Medicare Supplement Insurance (or Medigap) policies are offered by private insurance companies and provide additional coverage to help with the expenses Original Medicare doesn't pay for, such as copayments, coinsurance, and deductibles. A Medigap policy only supplements your Original Medicare benefits—it doesn't provide additional benefits (like a Medicare Advantage plan does).

Medicare Prescription Drug Donut Hole: Most Part D plans have a coverage gap referred to as the "donut hole." This means you pay out-of-pocket for your prescriptions (up to a yearly limit) after your plan spends a certain amount for covered drugs. Once you meet (spend up to) your yearly out-of-pocket limit, your plan picks back up, and your coverage gap ends. (The donut hole phases out by the year 2020.)

For complete Medicare information, visit medicare.gov and healthcare.gov.

Agents/Brokers

There are currently over 1,100 different healthcare policies in the U.S. With that much information and variance in coverage, sometimes it takes an expert to sort through the options with you and evaluate plans based on your needs.

Insurance agents or brokers are individuals or patient advocate groups who can recommend a plan that's the best fit for you, help you apply for financial assistance, and enroll you in a Qualified Health Plan (QHP) through the Marketplace.

Agents/brokers are licensed and regulated by the state and typically make commissions from insurers for enrolling consumers into plans. (Some only sell plans from certain insurers.)

If the difficulty of making your way through the complicated offerings of different insurance plans seems overwhelming—and it can—consider seeking the assistance of an agent/broker. The upside is you not only can save some stress and anxiety, but you can sometimes save money, too.

Private Insurance Plans/Individual Health Insurance Policies

Private insurance plans are available directly through insurance companies, agents, and brokers. You can choose to enroll in one of these plans if you don't receive coverage through your employer.

These plans are ACA-compliant and are regulated under state law. They cover pre-existing conditions and free preventive care and don't cap annual benefits. If you're enrolled in one of these plans, you won't be subject to the tax penalty (see page 78) for not having health coverage.

Private insurance plans aren't listed or offered on the Marketplace outside of the Open Enrollment period (see page 76). If you choose to purchase a plan outside the Marketplace (whether it's during Open Enrollment or not), you won't get any income-based premium tax credits or other savings. Some companies sell private plans outside the Open Enrollment period that provide the coverage needed to meet the ACA individual responsibility requirement that allows you to avoid paying the tax penalty. But you should know that some don't provide Minimum Essential Coverage (MEC).

You can find out if a particular plan meets the MEC requirement by looking at its summary of benefits and coverage.

You can contact an insurance company directly or purchase insurance plans online from online broker companies like eHealthinsurance.com or eInsurance.com.

STEP 3: SELECT THE LEVEL OF COST SHARING THAT MATCHES YOUR BUDGET AND NEEDS

The Marketplace offers five categories, including four "metal levels" that cover different percentages of the total costs for an average person's care. The category determines how you share costs with your insurance plan but doesn't affect the quality or amount of care you receive. Each category takes into account the plans' premiums, copayments, coinsurance, deductibles, and out-of-pocket maximums.

Categories and average percentages are as follows:

- **Catastrophic:** you pay >60%, and your plan pays <40%
- **Bronze:** you pay 40%, and your plan pays 60%
- **Silver:** you pay 30%, and your plan pays 70%
- **Gold:** you pay 20%, and your plan pays 80%
- **Platinum:** you pay 10%, and your plan pays 90%

Percentages are approximate, but the category you choose will give you a good ballpark figure for the amount you'll spend for essential benefits for the year. You're responsible for 100% of the cost of healthcare services up until the point you meet your deductible. After meeting your deductible, you pay your coinsurance amount (the percentage of the cost for a specific service). After you meet your plan's out-of-pocket maximum for the year, you won't pay any other costs for covered benefits.

You'll need to think through your expected healthcare needs to choose the level of cost sharing that best fits your circumstances. This can be difficult because healthcare needs can't always be predicted, but use your past medical history and experiences as a guide.

Some plans have a lower out-of-pocket expense but will have a higher monthly premium. The category names (based on the traditional value of the metals) indicate the expense of the monthly premium, which determines the level of the deductibles, copays, and coinsurance. As the monthly premium goes up, copays and deductibles go down.

If you anticipate frequent visits to your doctor and the need for regular prescriptions, a Gold or Platinum plan might be best for you. They have higher monthly premiums but lower deductibles, and you'll pay less of your total care costs.

If you don't frequently use health services or take prescriptions on a regular basis, you may want to opt for a Silver, Bronze, or Catastrophic plan. These plans cover less of your costs when you need care, but they'll cost you less per month.

If you qualify based on your income and household size for cost-sharing assistance from the government to save on out-of-pocket costs, a Silver plan will be your best-value option. If you're eligible for out-of-pocket savings, you can only receive these savings if you're enrolled in a Silver plan. This will essentially give you the lower out-of-pocket costs that come with a Gold or Platinum plan with a Silver plan premium payment.

A Bronze plan is designed for those who seek lower monthly payments and can tolerate a higher deductible. You may think that the lower monthly payment of a Bronze plan looks more attractive, but with its higher deductible, significant cash on hand may be needed quickly. But if you're young and apparently healthy, a Bronze plan might be the right choice for you. The fact is, good health saves you a lot of money. You may never have to satisfy that higher deductible to begin your benefits.

Catastrophic plans are only available to adults under age 30 or those who have a hardship exemption (see pages 79-80). These plans are designed to cover worst-case scenarios like a disease, accident, or serious illness. You'll pay a low monthly premium with a Catastrophic plan.

At the end of the day, if you need significant healthcare services during the year, you'll probably pay the same or similar out-of-pocket expenses whether you have a Bronze, Silver, Gold, or Platinum plan.

See healthcare.gov/apply-and-enroll/health-insurance-plans-estimator-overview for more information about plans and costs.

STEP 4: SELECT THE NETWORK AND THE SET OF RULES THAT GOVERN THAT NETWORK

A network is a group of pre-contracted providers with whom your insurance plan is partnered. Healthcare providers include hospitals, doctors, pharmacies, nursing homes, physical therapy, etc.—any entity that provides a covered healthcare benefit. These networks (EPOs, HMOs, PSOs, and PPOs) and their sets of rules matter because there can be severe financial costs for seeking care outside of the network of approved providers.

Managed healthcare

Managed healthcare essentially means an established network of doctors, specialists, hospitals, pharmacies, and other providers contracted together with an insurance company to provide coordinated services within a specific framework of rules. Exclusive Provider Organizations (EPOs), Health Maintenance Organizations (HMOs), Preferred Provider Organizations (PPOs), and Point-of-Service plans (POS) are managed care options. Insurance plans are designed to meet different needs and vary by price, physician access, expanse of the network, and the costs incurred by going outside the network.

All managed care plans have rules that restrict the providers you can see by having much higher copayments and coinsurance penalties for going out of the network, and the expenses you incur when you do aren't counted towards your yearly out-of-pocket maximum. Plan availability depends on where you live.

These are six basic differences between the rules governing networks:

- Requirement to have a primary care physician
- Requirement to obtain a referral to see a specialist or receive other services
- Requirement to have pre-authorization before receiving services
- Whether or not the plan covers the cost of out-of-network care
- The amount of cost sharing that's your responsibility out of network
- Whether or not you're responsible to file insurance claims and do paperwork

Types of managed care networks and their set of rules

Exclusive Provider Organization (EPO): An EPO plan only covers services provided within the plan's network (except in an emergency).

Health Maintenance Organization (HMO): Coverage is typically limited to services from providers who work for or are contracted by the HMO, and out-of-network care usually isn't covered (except in an emergency). Care is more integrated and focused on wellness and prevention. You may be required to live or work in an HMO's service area in order to receive coverage.

Point of Service (POS): You pay less with a POS plan if you stay within the plan's network. You're also required to obtain a referral from your primary care doctor before seeing a specialist.

Preferred Provider Organization (PPO): You pay less if you use the providers within a PPO network, but you can go outside the network without a referral (for an additional cost). PPOs are the most expensive because of the large network size and (usually) good out-of-network coverage. Expenses incurred for going out of network aren't counted towards your yearly out-of-pocket maximum.

STEP 5: SELECT THE INSURANCE PLAN

After you've done your research, choose an insurance plan that has 1) your doctor in its network, 2) an acceptable network, 3) acceptable network rules, and 4) the metal level that fits your financial situation and expected needs for the year.

OPEN ENROLLMENT PERIOD

One of the basic goals of the ACA is for as many people as possible to have health insurance. But it's not as simple as just buying insurance whenever you want—you can only sign up during the Open Enrollment period for each year. (Dates vary from year to year, but the 2016 Open Enrollment period begins November 1, 2015 and closes January 31, 2016.) When you sign up determines when your coverage begins. If you don't meet the enrollment deadline, you won't be able to enroll in a health insurance plan for that year unless you qualify for a Special Enrollment period.

Certain life change events and circumstances may qualify you for a Special Enrollment period. If you don't get health insurance, you may have to pay a tax penalty in addition to paying for all of your healthcare expenses. More information follows on penalties, exceptions, and exemptions.

SPECIAL ENROLLMENT PERIOD ELIGIBILITY

If you don't enroll during Open Enrollment, you must qualify for a special exception to be able to buy health insurance. The following life events may make you eligible for a Special Enrollment period:

- You turn 26 and lose coverage through a parent's insurance plan
- You get married
- You get divorced and were receiving your health insurance through your spouse's plan
- You have a baby, adopt a child, or place a child for adoption or foster care
- Your spouse/partner dies, leaving you without health insurance
- Your spouse/partner loses his/her job, and you had coverage through his/her employer
- You lose your job-based coverage (for any reason other than quitting a plan mid-year)
- You have coverage through a Marketplace plan but experience a change in income or household status that affects your eligibility for premium tax credits or cost-sharing reductions
- You lose Medicaid or CHIP eligibility (including a child passing the CHIP age limit)
- You move to a new residence
- You gain U.S. citizenship or lawful presence

- You leave incarceration

If you voluntarily drop your coverage mid-year, you won't qualify for a Special Enrollment period. The only time you can re-enroll is during Open Enrollment. You also don't qualify for mid-year re-enrollment if you lose coverage due to failure to pay your premium.

If you apply for a special exception and are rejected, you can appeal the decision to the Health Insurance Marketplace.

If you're eligible for enrollment in Medicaid or CHIP, you can enroll at any point during the year. If you qualify for either of these programs, your coverage can begin immediately.

If you're a member of a federally recognized Native American tribe or an Alaska Native shareholder, you may enroll in or change plans at any point during the year.

Your health insurance coverage will start only after you have made your first premium payment.

Visit healthcare.gov/coverage-outside-open-enrollment/ special-enrollment-period for other exceptions and complete details.

UNINSURED TAX PENALTY

All taxpayers must report their health insurance status from the previous year to the IRS. Most will check a box. The IRS will collect fines from some uninsured people and decide if others qualify for exemptions. If you don't buy insurance and don't have coverage, how much uninsured tax will you be required to pay?

In 2015, the tax penalty (based on a percentage of income) for not having health insurance increased to 2% of household income, and the flat dollar amount increased to $325 per adult and $162.50 per child under age 18. The IRS uses only the amount of income above the tax-filing threshold (approximately $10,150 for an individual) to calculate the penalty.

In 2016, these figures will increase to 2.5% of household income and $695 per adult ($347.50 per child under age 18). After 2016, the flat dollar amounts may increase with inflation.

You'll pay the fee on the federal income tax return you file for the year you don't have coverage. About 30 different kinds of waivers can help, most based on financial hardship.

Visit healthcare.gov/fees-exemptions/fee-for-not-being-covered for more information.

TAX EXEMPTIONS FROM UNINSURED TAX PENALTY

If you qualify for an exemption, you don't have to pay the fee for not having health coverage. Exemptions include reasons due to income, group membership, living abroad as a U.S. citizen, and hardship (explained in further detail in the following section). If your plan qualifies as Minimum Essential Coverage (MEC), you're covered under the healthcare law and aren't required to pay the fee or obtain an exemption.

Examples of MEC include any Marketplace plans (and most individual health plans bought outside the Marketplace), job-based plans (including retiree and COBRA coverage), Medicare (Part A or Part C), CHIP, most Medicaid coverage, coverage under a parent's plan for those under age 26, self-funded coverage offered to students by universities, certain veterans health coverage, most TRICARE plans, and Refugee Medical Assistance.

Visit healthcare.gov/fees-exemptions/plans-that-count-as-coverage for more details.

HARDSHIP EXEMPTIONS

Some exemptions from the tax penalty for failure to have health insurance are based on "hardships"—life situations that prevent you from obtaining coverage.

Any of the following may qualify you for a hardship exemption:

- You were recently homeless
- You were evicted within the last six months or faced eviction or foreclosure
- You recently received a utility shut-off notice
- You recently experienced domestic violence
- You recently experienced the death of a close family member
- You experienced a natural or human-caused disaster that caused significant damage to your property
- You filed for bankruptcy within the last six months

- You accumulated substantial debt from inability to pay for medical expenses within the last two years
- You experienced an unexpected financial burden from providing care for an ill, disabled, or elderly family member
- You were deemed ineligible for Medicaid because your state didn't expand eligibility under the ACA

Visit healthcare.gov/fees-exemptions/exemptions-from-the-fee for additional hardship exemptions, details, and application information.

HEALTH SAVINGS ACCOUNTS

A Health Savings Account (HSA) is a medical savings account option for taxpayers who have a high deductible insurance plan. These accounts are usually offered through your insurance company or employer. The money you deposit into this account is exempt from federal income tax, and account contributions are 100% tax deductible from gross income. This can amount to savings of 25% or more.

These funds are only available for qualified medical expenses. Many HSA plans give you a debit card to use when you pay for services. An HSA rolls over year to year—an attractive alternative to the "use it or lose it" Flexible Spending Account (FSA).

If you choose a lower monthly payment health plan, we recommend you deposit at least half of the monthly savings into your HSA. Even if you rarely get sick, you don't want to get caught off guard because you haven't made a habit of depositing regularly into your account. For example, if you choose a Bronze or Silver plan that gives you monthly savings of $500, put at least $250 of that into your HSA every month. This is a wise decision for a young, healthy individual to save money and be well prepared. Many small business owners choose to allocate the maximum amount to their account each year and save those accumulated funds for Medicare expenses later in life.

HSA holders can choose to save up to $3,350 for an individual and $6,650 for a family annually. HSA holders age 55 and older save an extra $1,000, which means $4,350 per individual and $7,650 per family.

See ustreas.gov for more information.

FEDERALLY QUALIFIED HEALTH CENTERS (FQHCS)

FQHCs are federally funded nonprofit centers or clinics operating in medically underserved areas and populations. These organizations offer primary care regardless of patients' ability to pay, and services are provided on a sliding fee scale. These centers are the best place for those living in the gap between Medicaid and federal subsidy eligibility to receive care.

FQHCs are considered private clinics that have met federal guidelines. If you can't pay for services, the government will cover the cost. If you have insurance, your insurance will work there as long as the center is within your plan's network. (See page 114 in Chapter 11 for more information on FQHCs.)

GRANDFATHERED HEALTH PLANS

Grandfathered plans are group plans or individual policies that were purchased on or before March 23, 2010, when the ACA was signed into law. These plans are exempt from many of the changes mandated by the ACA but can lose their status in the event they make substantial alterations that limit the covered benefits or increase consumers' costs. If a health plan has grandfathered status, this information must be disclosed in its plan details.

CADILLAC TAX

There was a day when a Cadillac was the most expensive car on the road. Those days are long past, but the name still connotes a product that costs more than an alternative, and certain highly comprehensive and costly employee-based healthcare plans meet that description. As a lesser-known provision of the ACA, the Cadillac Tax is designed to reduce the tax write-offs associated with employer-provided healthcare and reduce excess healthcare spending.

Under the provision, which goes into effect in 2018, employers have to pay a 40% tax on the costs of each employee's health insurance if it exceeds a certain threshold. For individual coverage the threshold is $10,200 per year and $27,500 per year for family coverage.

While the actual number of people affected will be relatively small, the Cadillac Tax has the potential to impact union benefits, large employers who have been historically generous with health benefits, and many federal, state, and local government employees.

ON THE CHANCE THAT YOU STILL MAY BE A BIT CONFUSED

As we mentioned at the beginning, healthcare insurance is, to say the least, a challenging topic. But it's the intersection where your finances and your health come together, so it's vitally important. If this rather large hit of information seems overwhelming now that you've gone through it, go back and read it again and keep this in mind: all of the material isn't relevant for every reader, so pick and choose the areas that are applicable to your specific situation. The whole point is to help you make informed decisions and understand the choices you have when it comes to selecting the right insurance plan for you and your family. You can also take a look at the appendix for additional information and access the National Underinsured/Uninsured Resource Directories.

Chapter 8:

THE MORE YOU KNOW: PATIENT ENGAGEMENT & BETTER HEALTH OUTCOMES

SEARCH ENGINE TRAFFIC HAS become a fairly common measurement of where certain topics fit in to our global conversation. At the time of this writing there were over 12 million results for the term "patient engagement," and there likely will be even more by the time you read this book. That kind of response may not be all that spectacular if you compare it to such areas as popular culture, politics, news, and sports. But it's pretty impressive in the world of healthcare.

If this term is new to you, don't feel like you haven't been paying attention. While patient engagement has been called, perhaps a little too dramatically, the "holy grail" of healthcare, it remains a relatively new concept that arose out of healthcare reform. The nonprofit Center for Advancing Health defines patient engagement as "the actions individuals must take to obtain the greatest benefit from the healthcare services available to them." You get the idea, but beyond that generality there doesn't seem to be universal agreement on any single explanation and no definitive sense of what it looks like in actual practice. What *is* clear is that patient engagement is an approach to personal healthcare that wouldn't have made the rounds in the days of paternalistic physicians who felt that "the doctor knows best" was the only rationale and motivation their patients needed.

While there may not be a single, precise definition for patient engagement, or at least a definition upon which everyone agrees, there are certain common characteristics: improved communication between providers and patients; a sense of partnership and shared decision making when it comes to things like approaches to care in general and treatment choices in particular; and people taking more responsibility for their health. Regarding that last point, there's an ongoing and growing body of research that indicates people who are more actively involved in their own health and healthcare experience improved outcomes. And in a related note that gets the attention of care providers and insurers, these same engaged people also incur lower healthcare costs.

While that's the good news about patient engagement, there are also some challenges. For example, it requires not only the motivation to be more informed and active, but also the ability. Because of health literacy (and general literacy), access to information, personal assertiveness, socio-economic disparities, and other factors, some people may simply not be able to participate in a greater degree of patient engagement, even if they're otherwise willing. These individuals will need more support to change behaviors and assimilate information, along with community health resources that make that possible. At the same time, the complexities and fragmentation of the healthcare system and the old-school traditions of some physicians can be a barrier to increased involvement. And then there's the fact that the "patient" part of the term itself (given that most people hopefully don't go around thinking of themselves as a patient) comes from the healthcare provider side of the engagement equation.

Patient engagement may not fall perfectly into the holy grail category, but it does promise to help usher in some needed changes in the way care is delivered and paid for as we shift from a fee-for-service model to a value-based approach. And those changes are already opening the door to four notable differences in healthcare.

1. DIFFERENT CONSUMERS

In the past, most of the interactions that took place in a physician's exam room were between an active doctor and a passive patient. There was no way for comparative shopping when it came to the cost of treatment, no means to get a "report card" or any type of background on the physician, and no easy access to health information to help you make knowledgeable decisions.

The internet has changed all that. Online resources offer in-depth information that can be particularly valuable when it comes to a wide range of health issues. The caution here is that the information you get needs to be reliable and accurate. Toward that end, government organizations like the National Institutes of Health, the Centers for Disease Control and Prevention, and healthfinder.gov are excellent sources of information.

You can also count on such resources as the Mayo Clinic's patient care and health information site, HealthTIPS from the American College of Physicians, and a variety of other sites. At the same time, keep in mind that there are some sources of online health information that range from misinformed to downright dangerous, so it's good to stick with the sites of highly-respected institutions and organizations.

As part of preparing this book, we spoke with Andrew Webber, the CEO of the Maine Health Management Coalition, who reminded us that there has traditionally been an "imbalance of power" between the information held by the people who need care and those who provide the service. In many ways, he added, the "white-coat culture of medicine" contributed to this gap with a physician-centric approach to care, as well as the fact that many people "actually want their doctors to make decisions for them rather than share in the process."

The imbalance between doctor and patient, which you could also look at as the difference between being passive and active about your health, is what you can help change by doing your homework. The point isn't to compete with the years of study, training, and experience your doctor has in diagnosing, treating, and managing health issues. It's simply to become more informed about determining health risks for specific diseases and conditions and the kinds of choices you can make to reduce those risks.

2. DIFFERENT MONEY

It might be nice to find a new analogy for the unsustainable economics of healthcare, but the old one works just fine. It's the tried and true image of the blank check. As consumers, most of us expected and sometimes demanded whatever care was needed to "fix" a situation, regardless of how we may have been contributing to the problem through lifestyle behaviors. It may have been nice while it lasted, but it seems that somebody suddenly took back the checkbook with all those blank checks.

As we discuss elsewhere in this book, the changes in the way healthcare is paid for, especially in regard to employer-based health insurance, are making it more expensive. That added expense generally takes the form of cost sharing, a percentage of healthcare costs that many employees pay out of their own pocket. Cost sharing typically includes deductibles (a flat amount that employees pay to be eligible for coverage), copayments (a fixed amount paid at the time services are obtained), and coinsurance (a percentage of costs that is typically billed after services are received).

Cost sharing can also include higher premium contributions that are usually taken out of an employee's paycheck. In all cases, the thinking is that the more people participate in their own care, including paying for it, the more likely they are to focus more on healthier (and less risky) lifestyles. In turn, these changes contribute to improving our health and lowering our healthcare costs as a nation.

Ultimately, the price we pay and the value we gain (literally and figuratively) for our healthcare coverage will be a positive difference in what has been a dysfunctional economic model.

3. DIFFERENT LIFESTYLES

Patient engagement is a key factor in taking more responsibility for your health, and nowhere does that responsibility yield greater results than in the area of lifestyle choices. Statistics show that seven of the top 10 causes of death in the U.S. are related to chronic diseases, conditions like heart disease, hypertension, certain cancers, diabetes, respiratory disease, oral conditions, and arthritis.

Other diseases that fall into this category include depression, obesity, renal (kidney) failure, and metabolic syndrome, a group of risk factors that come together to create potentially serious health concerns. Taken as a whole, these chronic conditions also account for the majority of healthcare spending in our country and affect almost one out of every two adults.

Traditionally, chronic disease has been treated problem by problem and episode by episode with a payment system that relied on volume to generate profit. The burden is enormous, both in human suffering and medical expenditures, which are borne by everyone through factors like higher insurance premiums, government expenditures, and disability benefits. And for the most part, it's unnecessary.

The alternative to this "put out the fire" approach is preventing or delaying the underlying causes of the chronic diseases, which in virtually every case involves clearly understood lifestyle choices such as smoking, overuse of alcohol, poor diet, lack of exercise, and inadequate relief of chronic stress. Conversely, people who replace these behaviors with comprehensive lifestyle modification—people who simply eat better, exercise more, and stop substance abuse for example—experience fairly rapid and meaningful improvements in health outcomes.

If better health begins with better information, this is the place to start. And learning more about the resources that can help you make the necessary lifestyle changes, through your own efforts and with the help of your familiar physician, is the very first step. And that's patient engagement at its best.

4. DIFFERENT CONVERSATIONS

Patient engagement is always going to be a little difficult to precisely nail down because it can take a number of forms. It can be, for example, a direct discussion of treatment options between a familiar physician and an informed patient. It can be looking at comparative information on the quality of hospitals, physicians, and specific medical procedures. Patient engagement can also be a candid conversation about the out-of-pocket costs of different treatment options.

On the organizational level it can be educational initiatives from healthcare and community organizations, as well as e-health tools and systems designed to direct consumer inquiries and support feedback. All of these efforts are going to take some additional efforts on the part of both the medical community and the public.

Our colleague, Dr. Debra Scammon, adjunct professor of Family and Preventive Medicine at the University of Utah, reinforces the idea that greater self-responsibility requires some highly focused and ongoing work on the patient's part. But she adds, "The payoff is worth it because while individuals benefit from their own personal investment in their health, there's an even bigger picture involved. A revolution in personal accountability could become the saving grace for our medical future. It's already happening right now. All over the nation we see consumers awakening to the absolute necessity of personal accountability for their health."

And while this initiative begins on a patient-by-patient basis, it's going to be supported by all of the stakeholders in healthcare—the patients, clinicians, employers, health plans, and community health programs—because everyone benefits from patient engagement. At its most basic level, the engagement begins at the moment when a person and his or her familiar physician begin a conversation that combines reliable information and professional advice.

EXPECTATIONS VS. REALITY

You should have high standards and expectations for your health and care providers. But now that you're taking a more active role in discussions and decisions about your health, we want to caution you about the danger of unreasonable expectations.

Some lifestyle changes will take time to adopt, some are non-negotiable, and some simply won't be possible for you and your specific circumstances. So you'll have to figure out which are right for you and realistic for your life.

The same is true for your expectations toward your doctor. He or she can't "fix" you or make you live a healthy life—that's not his or her job. A doctor can point you in the right direction, monitor your wellness or chronic conditions, and recommend medications and treatment, but can't guarantee results. And eventually he or she may make a mistake or error of judgment with your care.

That's right—every doctor makes mistakes at some point. Mistakes are inevitable in the real world. People and medicine can be difficult to figure out, and every case is unique. Rarely are these mistakes "gross negligence," and most often they fall somewhere within the "standard of care," a term that is generally taken to mean the treatment process that a "prudent" clinician should follow for a certain type of patient, illness, or circumstance. To avoid excessive costs, patients typically don't want every possible test to be done. The doctor doesn't want to waste your money, but neither does she or he want to risk making the wrong diagnosis. This is a point of conversation for the two of you, particularly since in some cases, you'll pay for the services until your insurance kicks in. Like other sciences there are some cases where there simply isn't a definitive right or wrong answer.

MAKE YOUR ENGAGEMENT A LONG-TERM COMMITMENT

With all those search engine hits we talked about, there's always the chance that patient engagement will turn out to be a media phenomenon or even one of those buzzwords that eventually fades into obscurity. But that's not very likely.

From everything we've personally experienced or have otherwise been exposed to, patient engagement is the real thing. As we stated earlier, the simple truth is that people who take more responsibility for their own health have better health outcomes and use fewer health resources. It's time to become one of those people.

Chapter 9:

MENTAL HEALTH: WHERE WE'VE BEEN AND WHERE WE'RE GOING

ON ONE HAND WE'VE come a long way. In the distant past many cultures viewed mental illness as a punishment from the gods or a demonic possession. In the less distant past and even up until the 1960s in our own country, individuals with mental health problems were confined, often un-hygienically and sometimes brutally, in state-run psychiatric facilities. As mass institutionalization gave way to more community-based mental healthcare, some of these situations clearly changed for the better.

On the other hand, with mental health issues now being part of a cause-and-effect relationship with conditions like homelessness, incarceration, suicide, and violence, with mental health budgets being the first to go when the economy weakens, and with societal stigmas that continue to follow people seeking care, we still have a long way to go.

SOME ROOM FOR CAUTIOUS OPTIMISM

It's been estimated that somewhere between one in five to six people experience some form of mental illness over the course of a year, including bipolar disorder, schizophrenia, or depression. In many cases symptoms are relatively mild, which is often true of depression, and don't impede day-to-day activities. Millions of people, however, suffer serious mental illness that greatly impacts their quality of life and affects their ability to function. The numbers are high, and the scope of illness is even more surprising. For example, the Diagnostic and Statistical Manual of Disorders (DSM), the American Psychiatric Association's standard reference and classification resource, listed over 450 mental disorders in its most recent edition.

Despite the pervasive nature of mental illness in our society, mental healthcare has always been in the shadows of the larger healthcare system. It's likely that only oral health has received less notice on our national radar. As part of this general inattention, access to mental healthcare lags behind other medical services, especially in more rural areas, and there's also a shortage of mental health professionals when compared to other types of care providers. In addition, the cost of mental health treatment and the fact that it hasn't traditionally been included in many health plans has created a barrier to utilization.

At least some of the optimism we mentioned stems from the increased focus on mental healthcare in the Affordable Care Act. As specifically detailed within the law, the ACA requires all insurers who sell on the Health Insurance Marketplace (also known as the exchanges) to include mental health and substance use disorder treatment benefits in their coverage packages. These mandates build on earlier legislation that we'll talk about shortly.

While mental healthcare remains an imperfect system with unmet needs across the whole spectrum of care, improvements are coming. And even now there's a wide range of services and resources available within the community to you and your family.

TOOLS, RESOURCES, AND HOPE

In emergency departments across the country, physicians respond to mental health crises every day, and most hospitals have a 24-hour walk-in evaluation team. The network of mental health services in the U.S. includes collaborative partnerships between private psychiatric hospitals and publicly-funded community mental health centers. There are also school-based (primary and secondary) health clinics that provide mental healthcare and substance abuse counseling.

In addition, the overall mental health network offers a large number of psychiatrists, psychologists, therapists, and clinical social workers for private and group counseling. And community-led organizations like Alcoholics Anonymous and Narcotics Anonymous, as well as nonprofit and faith-based organizations, offer other options for resources and support. We'll discuss some of these later in a little more detail.

One important measure of improvement centers around the fact that in the past, mental health services never matched up with conventional medical coverage. In 2008, the Mental Health Parity and Addiction Equality Act created new regulations regarding healthcare coverage for mental health services and substance use disorder treatment. As mentioned, the ACA then built on this original legislation.

Taken together, these laws represent a major shift from the minimal mental health insurance coverage of the past. The "parity" part of the legislation, which is also picked up in the ACA, means that mental health and substance abuse coverage have to be on par with the coverage offered for other medical care. Large group health plans for companies with more than 50 employees, small group health plans, and individual market plans are required to cover mental health and substance use disorder services equivalent to the level of coverage of medical and surgical benefits.

WHAT DO YOU DO IF YOU'RE IN THE MIDDLE OF A MENTAL HEALTH CRISIS?

A mental health or substance abuse crisis doesn't necessarily mean there's a risk of danger to self or others, but behaviors that pose immediate harm should always be met with an emergency response. Keep in mind that what professionals characterize as a mental health crisis can look much different if it's taking place in your living room. While there's no one-size-fits-all crisis, situations can include intense personal distress (things like depression, anger, anxiety, panic), changes in functioning (this could be any number of unusual behaviors, including something as basic as neglect of personal hygiene), or a catastrophic life event (including being victimized by another person, disruption in a personal relationship or living situation, and loss of autonomy or parental rights).

If you're in the physical presence of a friend or family member who is experiencing a crisis—or if you're in communication with him or her—you should call 911 or take the individual to the hospital. The law in most states allows a friend or family member to become involved if the person in crisis permits it. If he or she gives permission, emergency responders can exchange information with the friend or family member. Of course, someone experiencing a true mental health crisis may not be willing or able to give permission, so a 911 call may be the best course of action.

Parental/guardian consent is required before another person can become involved in a minor's mental health crisis. If a parent/guardian doesn't accompany the child to the hospital, the medical staff can't share privileged medical information until a parent/guardian gives permission.

An experienced emergency response team should know how the law applies to each case and will help walk you through the right steps. The most important thing you can do is help the person in need get access to care as quickly as possible.

ADDITIONAL THOUGHTS ON WHERE TO TURN IN A CRISIS

As part of the development of this book, we spoke with Craig Nuckles, retired regional vice president of behavioral health at Universal Health Services based in King of Prussia, Pennsylvania. Craig shared the following guide with us, which provides some additional direction for accessing mental health services in the event of a crisis situation:

- *If an individual seeks help on a voluntary basis, go with him or her to a psychiatric hospital or a nearby acute care hospital Emergency Room. In addition to their own medical staff, a number of hospitals have contracts with psychiatric service providers to see patients in their ERs.*

- *Some community or county health centers have emergency walk-in services (which may not be operating 24/7) and in some cases a mobile crisis unit with clinical staff able to make an on-site evaluation of a person's condition.*

- *If the individual has a psychiatrist or is being treated by another mental health professional, call this individual to inform him or her of the situation and to receive guidance.*

- *Hospital Emergency Rooms are required by law to provide mental health assessment and stabilization services regardless of the ability to pay. Any opportunity (which may not be possible in a crisis situation) to research the facility is helpful as treatment capabilities vary between hospital providers. While many hospitals have excellent psychiatric units, the specialization available through a psychiatric hospital can be beneficial, particularly in crisis situations. Note that the term "Behavioral Health" is often used interchangeably with mental health, particularly in hospital settings. In researching resources, you may find that facilities refer to the "Behavioral Health Center" as the primary treatment center for mental health issues.*

- *As you would expect, involuntary care complicates the picture. If the individual has a weapon of any kind and threatens to use it or has ingested a quantity of pills or other dangerous chemicals, call 911.*

- *If individuals persistently report hearing voices or having visions directing them to hurt themselves or others, contact the local court system for direction to the division that handles mental illness warrants. This type of court order authorizes law enforcement officials to take a person into custody for a mental illness that includes being at immediate and serious risk for harm to self and others. The courts rarely view simply experiencing hallucinations as a crisis, and any dangerous situation must be happening in the present. Past behaviors won't be considered for a warrant.*

- *Remember that mental health experts define a person in crisis as someone who is imminently suicidal or homicidal with the means to carry out the action or psychotic with intent to harm self or others. Chemically dependent/alcoholic individuals can also fall in to this category if they have a history of withdrawal.*

- *In most states, parents/guardians have the right to hospitalize their children against their will if the child meets those criteria. If unable to manage their involuntary child, the parent/guardian should call 911.*

CONSIDER THESE RESOURCES FOR NON-CRISIS SITUATIONS

Community-based counseling

Community mental health centers typically provide short and long-term counseling services for children, adolescents, and adults. These services can vary in scope based on location. Some community mental health centers also include geriatric programs, which can also be of value to the adult children of older adults. Because of the funding mechanism for state or county programs, some may run out of money near the end of their fiscal year (usually in the summer), so certain services may be limited.

Federally Qualified Health Centers (FQHCs), which were developed to provide a broad range of healthcare for historically underserved populations, include mental healthcare provided on a sliding scale (based on income). Patients can get help from a psychologist, clinical social worker, or another individual who's trained to provide some degree of mental health services.

Be aware that most FQHCs don't have a psychiatrist (a medical doctor specializing in the diagnosis and treatment of mental disorders) on staff.

There are also many private counseling centers that offer counseling and psychological services to children and adults in an outpatient setting.

Alcoholics Anonymous and Narcotics Anonymous

Alcoholics Anonymous (AA) and Narcotics Anonymous (NA) are nonprofit, international, community-based organizations that offer recovery programs in a group atmosphere with an ongoing peer support network. These groups are open to everyone at no cost.

Visit aa.org or na.org to learn more or find a group near you.

Nonprofit and faith-based groups

Nonprofit and faith-based groups help fill the treatment gap when public programs are not readily available or preferred. Services vary but generally include a range of resources and support for individuals and families. They're usually privately funded through donations, grants, and some income generation, as well as public sector funding in some cases. Groups affiliated with a local faith-based community often have particular expertise with teens and youth recovery programs as well as family counseling.

Probably the single most important point to remember about mental health services is that like other aspects of our health, it's best to be proactive. Don't wait until there's a crisis to reach out for help. The sooner you or a loved one can find the services or support needed—for any mental or substance use disorder concerns—the better. And the less likely you'll be to need more intensive levels of care down the road.

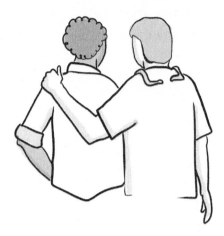

THE BRIDGE BETWEEN MENTAL HEALTH AND PRIMARY CARE

One of the lasting takeaways we hope you derive from reading this book is the role of primary care medicine as the foundation of a healthcare system capable of improved quality and lower costs. As part of that objective, it's important to point out what primary care providers have always known: mental health is a major public health issue and a comorbidity (a disease or condition that occurs simultaneously with the primary condition being treated) in many people seen by the primary care team. In fact, research indicates that depression as a comorbidity with chronic disease occurs in up to 40% of the population being treated.

At the same time, people with mental illness have a higher mortality rate and often die prematurely due to preventable diseases such as diabetes, cardiovascular disease, and respiratory diseases. Persons living with serious mental illness also have a higher rate of high-risk behaviors, including smoking, lack of exercise, poor nutrition, obesity, unsafe sexual behavior, alcohol consumption, and drug use.

What this scenario ultimately means is that the people served by our health system will receive a higher level of care and experience improved health outcomes when mental health, viewed without stigma or a sense of separation, is fully integrated into the larger sphere of healthcare.

SOME HELPFUL LINKS

psychiatry.org/mental-health/more-topics/insurance-and-parity

"Practice Guidelines: Core Elements in Responding to Mental Health Crises" store.samhsa.gov/shin/content/ SMA09-4427/SMA09-4427.pdf

Chapter 10:

HEALTHCARE AT THE END OF LIFE

YOU KNOW THE FAMOUS Benjamin Franklin quote about nothing being certain except death and taxes? Well, it's time to talk about one of those certainties, and not being accountants, we don't have much to say about taxes. We *will* be talking about that other topic though. For many people, it can end up being a highly emotional and unpleasant conversation. But it's one we need to have, because death frequently has a close relationship to our healthcare system in terms of both human and financial burdens.

As a measure of how difficult discussions about death really are, we tend to use the phrase "end-of-life" care, which really isn't all that successful in sugar coating the reality. Regardless of the terminology, the medical profession doesn't exhibit its finest hour when it comes to mortality issues, at least with regards to communicating about them. And there may be some good reasons why.

REFLECTIONS ON A JOB *NOT* WELL DONE

If you think of it purely in terms of a physician's professional achievement, the end of life for a patient can represent a sense of failure. For people trained and motivated to improve health and sustain life, being unable to change the course of a disease through skills, experience, and technology may be seen as an example of simply not getting the job done—at least if you're looking at dying as a medical problem to be solved rather than a universal human condition and one of the most profound of personal experiences.

The result is that the aggressive treatment sometimes provided in the final months, weeks, or days of life doesn't always correlate with the values and preferences of the patient and family. Then there's that very human trait we share about not liking to deliver and then continue discussing bad news, and death and dying usually rank at the top of the bad news category. While other factors are at play in the way end-of-life issues are sometimes mishandled, a good part of the problem remains related to communication.

For example, and we discussed this issue earlier with regard to medical care in general, some physicians concentrate on physical symptoms at the expense of the mental, spiritual, and emotional components of health. Given that particular focus, which in some cases is carried out over many years of care, it's unrealistic to expect that doctors would suddenly change their approach at the end of a patient's life. We should add on behalf of those doctors that it isn't necessarily that they don't want to listen to patients and families. More likely, they haven't received the kind of training that helps them know what to listen for.

Surgeon and author Dr. Atul Gawande noted this deficit in the introduction to his book, *Being Mortal,* an exceptional meditation on aging and death that we highly recommend. In describing his experience as a med student, he expressed a thought with which we as physicians strongly concur: "I learned a lot of things in medical school, but mortality wasn't one of them."

On that front there's some good news in that medical students and residents are now receiving more guidance in end-of-life care, and there are excellent training programs and communication techniques available for practicing physicians. There are also recently developed fellowship programs in palliative and hospice care, two fields that will increasingly make their presence felt in the end-of-life areas of medicine.

COMFORT, COMPASSION, AND QUALITY OF LIFE

If death and dying were purely financial considerations rather than an inevitable and natural part of the human condition, there would be a pretty good argument against them. In both the public and private sectors, a high percentage of healthcare dollars are spent on end-of-life care. Medicare estimates that 25% of its payments are directed to the last year of a beneficiary's life with the majority paid out during the final two months. That might be a good use of the money if it was actually helping patients in some meaningful way to minimize suffering and maximize quality of life.

Instead, much of it goes toward critical care therapies, often related to multiple organ failures that help people live neither better nor much longer. At the same time, this costly treatment can use up personal savings for copays and non-covered services, leaving surviving family members with even more problems. (*On a very personal note, co-author Dr. Grundy remembers, "The money spent on my dad's healthcare in a short time before he died was more than he made in his entire life as a missionary."*)

Within this context, the emergence and continuing rise of palliative care and hospice care represent a far better solution for society as a whole, individual patients and their families, and the medical profession.

PALLIATIVE CARE

This relatively new medical specialty was developed for people with serious, chronic, and life-threatening illnesses. It focuses on improving life and providing comfort through pain management and relief of symptoms like nausea, shortness of breath, insomnia, fatigue, loss of appetite, and depression that often accompany severe illness. Palliative care uses a team of health professionals that typically includes primary care and specialty physicians, nurses, physical and occupational therapists, psychologists or psychiatrists, social workers, dieticians, and chaplains. Once this multidisciplinary team is in place, it provides services that transcend conventional medical care.

Unlike hospice care, which we'll look at shortly, palliative care is appropriate at any stage of serious illness and can be used in tandem with treatments that are working toward a cure or improved management of a condition. In other words, people receiving palliative care may still have hope for recovery. In many cases, it helps patients better tolerate curative treatment, including difficult side effects. As a result, people can move in and out of palliative care as the need arises.

If the cure of a life-threatening condition is not possible, palliative care can continue to improve quality of life. As the end of life approaches, it can provide a more seamless transition into hospice care.

HOSPICE CARE

At least for now, the number of hospice services far outnumbers the resources for palliative care. Speaking of which, palliative care forms an important core of hospice care, providing comfort, pain relief, and symptom management to people who are terminally ill. There's generally a broader range of services in hospice care. It began in nursing homes or specially equipped hospice facilities but has since grown more as an in-home service with an emphasis on bereavement and other counseling and related support for the patient's family.

The most important difference between palliative and hospice care is that in the latter, the illness has progressed to the point when curative treatment is no longer beneficial. In addition, hospice programs place more reliance on family caregivers and friends, supported by health professionals including a visiting hospice nurse.

Also, while the time period for palliative care is generally open ended, hospice patients must be considered to be terminal, usually within six months of death, in order to be eligible for insurance benefits. Regarding that issue, hospice care is paid for by Medicare, Medicaid in most states, the Department of Veterans Affairs, and most private insurance plans. Also, many hospice programs provide free or sliding-scale services for people who have difficulty affording them.

The basic philosophy behind hospice care is that by making the decision to forgo curative or life-prolonging treatment, individuals in hospice and their families can focus on getting the most out of the time that's left. The result is a greater opportunity to leave this world with as much dignity and comfort as possible.

In both palliative and hospice care every experience is unique, and every family dynamic is distinctive. What you or a family member should always express in either form of care is what your preferences are, what your goals are, and whether you have any religious or cultural traditions that could guide the care you hope to receive.

SOME BASIC CONSIDERATIONS AND QUESTIONS

In the midst of the emotional, spiritual, and profoundly personal aspects of serious illness, death, and dying, there are some unavoidable practical matters, too. For example, discussions about end-of-life issues and the planning that goes into them are more effective when they're carried out before a crisis arrives. With regard to end-of-life decisions, here are some general questions you may want to consider:

- *What's most important to you when you think about the closing stages of your life?*
- *Where do you want to be cared for in your final days?*
- *Do you want physicians to do everything possible to extend your life?*
- *What kind of life-sustaining or life-prolonging treatment—things like CPR, mechanical venting, intubation, long-term feeding through a tube, artificial hydration—do you want, if any?*
- *If additional treatments offer little possibility of benefit, do you want to continue receiving aggressive treatment care?*

IT'S NEVER TOO SOON TO MAKE A PLAN

The questions you just looked at are the first step in helping you to think through the issues involved. They can also help guide your conversations with your loved ones so they can share their wishes with you as well. But at some point you have to make a plan that is clearly spelled out and documented. Keep in mind; this isn't just for older adults. As the Greek playwright Euripides said, "No man can confidently say he will be living tomorrow," so despite your hopefully vibrant state of health, now is the time to make your wishes known.

The heart of advance healthcare planning is made up of what is known as advance directives, and there are two basic types, both of which you should have:

A LIVING WILL

A living will is a written document that lets doctors and other healthcare providers know the kind of medical treatment you want if you are dying or in a permanent coma and can't make decisions for yourself about emergency treatment. Specifically it spells out the procedures, like the ones we mentioned earlier, that you do or don't want and the conditions under which your choices would apply.

DURABLE POWER OF ATTORNEY FOR HEALTHCARE

This is a legal document naming a health proxy, someone whom you trust to make medical decisions for you if you're incapacitated. For obvious reasons, your proxy should be familiar with your wishes related to treatment decisions. While a durable power of attorney for healthcare enables you to be more specific than a living will and can theoretically take the place of one, it's a good idea to have both as an added measure of protection. Both documents, a living will and a durable power of attorney, can be obtained from your physician and do not require the involvement of an attorney.

ORDERS FOR LIFE-SUSTAINING TREATMENT

In addition to the traditional advance care planning documents, a growing number of states are now using a form known as POLST (Physician Orders for Life-Sustaining Treatment) or MOLST (Medical Orders for Life-Sustaining Treatment). Once completed and signed by your doctor, these forms have the same status as any other medical order.

The POLST document guides the patient's medical team regarding specific treatment options for specific conditions and is placed prominently in the medical record so healthcare providers will always be aware of the patient's choices and preferences. POLST doesn't exist in all states yet, so be sure to contact your state department of health or state medical association to see if your state has a program. If not, advocate that one be created, because they can be an extremely valuable as part of your advance care planning.

IT ALL COMES BACK TO THE FAMILIAR PHYSICIAN

Remember our discussion of the familiar physician—a primary care doctor who has cared for you over time and has an understanding of you as both a patient and a person? Well, end-of-life discussions are the perfect time to get that clinician involved. Your familiar physician can help walk you through the process of making the decisions that are right for you and your family. She or he can bridge the gap between medicine and the unique circumstances of your life and help you look at options. Most importantly, your familiar physician can provide the knowledge as well as the comfort and continuity that makes difficult and complex issues seem a little easier to face.

Chapter 11:

WHAT'S TRIED, TRUE, AND TRENDING IN HEALTHCARE

THERE'S AN OLD SAYING about education that reminds us that what we learn isn't intended to fill a container, but rather to light a fire. Lighting that fire, creating the interest to dive a little bit deeper into the areas of healthcare that interest you, is what this section is all about. We live in a time when information abounds and is easy to come by. The objective is to make certain (or as certain as you can) that it comes from an established, reliable, and updated source. Becoming a smart consumer of health information is the first step toward being a smart consumer of healthcare itself. So light a fire, get introduced to, and then learn more about the interesting and valuable profiles in this overview.

CONCIERGE MEDICINE AND DIRECT PRIMARY CARE: A NEW RELATIONSHIP WITH YOUR PRIMARY CARE DOCTOR

Concierge Medicine centers on receiving medical services from a PCP in which the payment model is a direct contract between you and your doctor. Basically you become part of a premium healthcare group for a cost that can range widely, usually $100-$1000 per month. This cost is typically paid by some combination of you or your employer (insurance is still filed for appropriate services and is part of the payment) and gives you virtually immediate access to your doctor through direct phone and email contacts. The office visits are longer and more focused, and the additional source of income means your doctor can decrease his or her patient population so you get more time and availability.

To give you an idea of the difference, concierge physicians care for somewhere between 50-600 patients compared to 2,000-3,000 patients for a traditional primary care practice. As a result, concierge practices are best known for careful physician attention, especially for chronic disease patients and the overall close management of health through frequent visits, monitoring, and personal encouragement.

Direct Primary Care is a form of Concierge Medicine that balances a heavier patient load (heavier than Concierge Medicine but still much lighter than a conventional practice) on the part of the doctor with lower monthly fees. In some cases, employers can contract directly with these practices instead of going through the normal route with an insurer. The employer then offers this Direct Primary Care option to the employees as a means of accessing primary care for free or drastically reduced office visit fees. The employer often pays the participation membership fees on behalf of the employee to the Direct Primary Care practice.

For a flat fee every month, patients have extensive access to their doctor in person or through phone, text, or email for all routine primary care services. This form of payment model does not rely on insurance copays, deductibles, or coinsurance fees. Direct Primary Care practices, without any additional insurance payment, offer physician services for a fee currently ranging from $30-$120 per month (fees will vary depending on the location). In addition to the straightforward direct care model, a number of hybrids also exist.

Pros and cons include, on the plus side, the fact that participants in a concierge or direct care relationship with their doctor gain significantly greater access for their medical needs through a payment system that also can give the doctor an improved work-life balance. On the downside, while it's good for the members, it's not so good for everyone else. With an existing and even greater shortage of PCPs on the horizon, reducing patient loads for the few places even greater demands on the many.

MEDICAL TRAVEL: THE ROAD TRIP THAT PAYS OFF

The U.S. has become one of the top three destinations worldwide for medical travel, receiving as many as 800,000 international patients each year. And there are a lot of good reasons for the travel. Now, as it turns out, U.S. residents are doing some traveling on their own on a purely domestic level. By going to other states and regions of our country, with the help of their employers, they're finding more cost-effective options for a wide range of procedures and treatment.

A growing number of large companies—usually self-insured—including Wal-Mart and Lowes, now offer medical travel as a healthcare benefit for employees, an innovation which can reduce healthcare costs while simultaneously providing high-quality care. The travel "destinations" are typically top-rated medical centers that have demonstrated superior outcomes with lower complications in specialized areas of care like cardiovascular procedures or back surgery. The company generally pays all out-of-pocket insurance costs and will often cover the costs of sending a caregiver as well.

In addition to their leading cost and quality indicators, the medical centers that take part in the program generally bundle all the physician and hospital charges into one price for the employer. This can end up being much less costly than performing the procedure locally, even when transportation and accommodations are included. These medical travel programs have produced a high rate of satisfaction among employers who negotiate for reduced costs, as well as among employees who save on deductibles and copays.

The site below offers an indication of the potential savings by comparing costs for the same procedure in different locations. The cost variances are surprisingly wide. Be aware that the medical travel option isn't remotely widespread yet, but it's growing. If you have the comparative information, you may be able to negotiate something with your employer even if there's no formal program.

bcbs.com/healthofamerica: "A Study of Cost Variation for Percutaneous Coronary Interventions (Angioplasties) in the U.S."

VBID: A GREAT WAY TO GET PAID FOR MAKING HEALTHIER DECISIONS

Discussions about health insurance tend to bring on either yawns or anxiety, so we'll explain value-based insurance design (VBID) as painlessly as possible. Let's say you're going to have a colorectal screening, maybe not your first choice of things to do, but an excellent example of where the relatively small cost of preventive care can save lives and considerable amounts of money later on. So in a VBID system your employer (at least for now most VBID plans are employer-based) will pay for most or all of that screening, because as we just stated, it saves money in the long run. *(Note that many insurance packages, including most of those purchased on the Health Insurance Exchange, already cover a range of preventive services of which colorectal screenings are included, but we're using it anyway for the sake of comparison.)*

Now, let's change it around a bit. You have some pain in your back, and you want to get an MRI with the expectation of spinal surgery. People with severe back pain want relief whatever the cost, but it turns out that for certain procedures, more conservative treatment offers equal or sometimes even more relief and function at a fraction of the cost. In this case, the employee who insists on the surgery can get the procedure but will pay a significantly higher share of the costs. The basic setup is that instead of all out-of-pocket costs being the same for the insured person, potentially life-saving tests and other high-value services will have reduced or no copays or deductibles as a way to distinguish them from procedures that may not be necessary.

So what we have is added support for consumers who make informed and more cost effective choices. In this way VBID encourages the use of services where the benefits exceed the cost—as determined through the evaluation and analysis of a large body of data and evidence-based medicine. It also provides economic incentives for making healthy lifestyle changes and rewards people who improve their health by losing weight or quitting smoking.

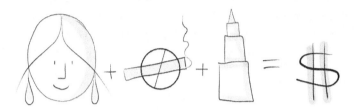

Value Based Insurance Design

As a logical next step, VBID will hopefully one day cover employee contributions for all primary care visits at reduced or eliminated cost while also providing medications for chronic conditions like high blood pressure or diabetes at no charge. While this extension of the concept may seem futuristic, its effectiveness is evidenced by the fact that a VBID plan with this level of benefits is already in place at IBM.

WHEN LOWER-COST HEALTHCARE STILL COSTS TOO MUCH

Using a single word to describe healthcare in America may bring some different choices to mind, but it seems that "expensive" is going to be near the top of anyone's list. We've offered some recommendations for controlling and lowering healthcare costs through a number of strategies, but there are times when that understandably isn't quite enough. For that reason, we've included directories at the back of this book as a special guide for people who are uninsured or underinsured. Regarding this particular issue, however, it never hurts to be reminded again that there are options.

Federally Qualified Health Centers (FQHCs)

These community-based resources provide affordable healthcare, including dental, prenatal, mental health, preventive care, and pharmacy services for millions of Americans in both rural and urban areas, which have been historically underserved by the healthcare system. They also play a crucial role in establishing primary care medicine as the foundation of our healthcare system. In addition, FQHCs assist uninsured patients with enrollment into Medicaid, CHIP, and other assistance programs. FQHCs operate on a sliding scale payment model, based on income and ability to pay.

For more information on FQHCs and to find one in your area, visit the following site: findahealthcenter.hrsa.gov/Search_HCC. aspx

Free clinics

Free and charitable medical clinics have a long history of serving as a safety net for people who fall through the cracks of the healthcare system, and there have often been quite a few cracks. The healthcare professionals who make up the staff include many volunteers, while medical supplies and expenses are covered by philanthropy and fundraising. Some free clinics receive small amounts of operating funds through state or federal grants, but most do not. Services vary but often include primary care, dental care, OB/GYN services, pediatric care, audiology, health education and nutrition, vision care, urgent care, substance abuse counseling, and more.

Many free clinics may charge a nominal registration fee, as well as small charges for certain services. Free clinic personnel may also request an "intake" appointment to determine financial qualifications.

To learn more about free clinics and their locations, visit needymeds.org/inclusions/free_clinics_branch.htm or nafcclinics.org.

SOME THOUGHTS ON HOME AND AGING

Fueled in large part by increasing life expectancies, it's estimated that by 2030 one out of every five adults will be 65 years of age or older. And that's going to change everything. It already has. Overall services, older adult housing options, specialized medical care, lifestyle opportunities, and a wide array of assistive, age-related technology have grown exponentially in the past couple of decades.

One day someone will look back and describe this "silver tsunami" as a culture-changing phenomenon that on some level will rewrite American social history. But our goals are decidedly more modest. What we want to convey is simply that you need to plan for it, and that includes considering how your living situation may change as you grow older. Because according to the actuarial tables, many of you reading this now will be here to reap the rewards from that planning.

Looking for a home

Housing for older adults used to be a fairly simple proposition. You stayed in your home as long as you could, and when you couldn't live there independently anymore, you moved in with an adult child or other relative. Things have gotten a lot more interesting. While the basic categories—independent living, assisted living, and skilled nursing care—are understandable enough, the subsets of each area create at least a dozen different choices. Even the old standby of remaining in your own home, also called "aging in place," has been enhanced through a wide range of support services that make for a safe and more comfortable experience.

To get a sense of these choices, which are usually made on factors like personal preference, health and mobility, overall capabilities, and finances, just plug "housing options for senior living" into your favorite search engine and get ready for an information overload. The residential options in the information from eldercare.gov and AARP alone will keep you busy for hours. It's always helpful to look through this material with other family members, and some of the choices may require legal advice.

Although planning sometimes runs counter to certain people's nature, we can't emphasize enough how important it is to be aware of what's out there as soon as possible and definitely before you need to make a decision. That's true for the individuals who'll be primarily affected by the decision, as well as those adult children whose lives may also be impacted.

LONG-TERM CARE INSURANCE: A GOOD DEAL OR NOT?

If you're looking ahead with the thought that being on Medicare will be your substitute for long-term care insurance, keep in mind that it only covers very short-term care in a skilled nursing facility—also called a nursing home or convalescent center. On the other hand, while the Medicaid program does cover long-term care, it has very strict requirements related to the assets you can have, as well as the income you can make.

Given that, consider these two scenarios. Number one finds you in a nursing home. You had a stroke, and the care you're receiving now is burning through your retirement savings, your life savings really, at a pretty furious rate. That's because nursing homes average around $50,000 a year—much more in some states—and costs are going up everywhere. At some point all your assets are gone. Once you recover, you find that your quality of life has changed dramatically for the worse. You become a burden on your family. You should have had long-term care insurance.

In scenario number two, in an effort to protect your hard-earned savings, you bought long-term care insurance when you were still working. After you retired, the premiums go up drastically (must have been something in that fine print) and become too much to pay, since your earnings in retirement are a lot less than when you were working. Plus, as it turns out, you've been healthy and living comfortably in your home the whole time. Buying that long-term care insurance was an expensive mistake.

You get the idea. It's all about risk management or how lucky you feel. Fortunately, there are quite a few sources, including AARP and *Consumer Reports* that offer some solid information about the pros and cons of long-term care insurance and can provide you with unbiased guidance in making a decision. We're not going to take a stance, because only you can weigh those pros and cons and be aware of your own personal circumstances. But we will predict the future just a bit.

Healthcare itself is evolving to less costly care sites, including a continual shift toward outpatient care. There's a good possibility that long-term care will mirror this trend as much as possible, and even services like skilled nursing care will be carried out in less expensive settings, including private homes. In fact, in 20 or 30 years, give or take, long-term care in general and skilled nursing care in particular may look quite a bit different—and the whole issue of long-term care insurance as we know it will take on a different set of criteria.

DIGITAL TECHNOLOGY: BUILDING BRIDGES BETWEEN PEOPLE AND HEALTHCARE

Distance is one of the barriers that has traditionally kept people, whole populations in some cases, from receiving the medical care they need. Time is another one of the classic roadblocks. The problem is that it's not always physically possible to get to where the best source of care is, and even when it is possible, it may not be convenient. Add the issue of transportation and face-to-face encounter costs to that equation, and you hit the trifecta of reasons why people sometimes can't or don't access needed care or better manage existing conditions, especially chronic diseases.

The good news there is that technology, more precisely a mix of advancements in digital communications, biomedicine, nanotechnology, telemetry, cloud computing, and human instrumentation, has removed many of the traditional impediments that once stood in the way of effective, easily accessed, and affordable care.

Telemedicine

Imagine seeing and talking with a highly trained physician specialist who just happens to be hundreds of miles away from where you are. Now imagine having that distant specialist direct the diagnostic study or treatment you need. That's telemedicine.

Picture a doctor in a rural community being able to consult, in real time, with a specialist at a major urban medical center while both of them simultaneously listen to your heartbeat, examine a suspicious mole on your shoulder, or work together to provide life-saving treatment for a stroke. That's telemedicine, too.

In its most basic form, telemedicine is the real-time, interactive communication between a patient and a care provider or care team at one location and a consulting physician or care team at a distant location. Telemedicine makes use of sophisticated teleconferencing technology along with specialized medical peripherals, a growing range of digital tools that can assess a patient's condition remotely. Much of the advanced technology came out of the care provided for members of the armed forces serving in remote places, as well as from the medical support available to crew members of space shuttle flights or International Space Station assignments.

While early telemedicine was focused more on the simple two-way exchange of data and diagnostic images, current capabilities include such areas as wound care, sleep studies, genetics counseling, dermatology, ENT, e-visits from nurses and doctors, psychology, maternity (tele-delivery), ophthalmology, and a variety of emergency triage and patient transfer situations. One of the more innovative forms of telemedicine involves remotely directed surgery using robotic surgical systems.

In all of these applications, the ability of telemedicine to "bring the doctor to the patient" not only increases convenience and comfort while lowering costs, it offers access to a level of care that otherwise might not be available.

Mobile measurement and monitoring devices

While some people may wear them as a fashion statement, many of the wristbands, pendants, headsets, and headbands you see in ever-increasing numbers are doing some important work. From wearable fitness monitoring as simple as a measurement of steps walked and calories burned, to portable consumer devices that can monitor vital signs like blood pressure, heart rate, blood oxygen saturation, respiration, blood glucose levels, and even brain waves, to clothes with sensors that record muscle function, a whole new world of personal healthcare has quickly come into being. Equally noteworthy, it's here to stay, because this particular revolution is helping people improve their health by adopting relatively simple behaviors that can positively impact their health in some cases and by seeking out appropriate clinical care in others.

We're not particularly qualified to speak to the various technologies involved except to say that the sensors beings used and the mobile devices they wirelessly "report to" (whether they are personal or healthcare system-based) are getting more sophisticated, more capable, and more accurate at a rapid pace. What we can talk about, however, is what it all means to you and your health, as well as your relationship with your health team.

To begin with, these measurement and monitoring devices are highly effective in helping people increase their awareness on a wide range of health issues in which fitness is only the beginning—though a very important one. In the long run, this technology has the ability, probably more than any force that has developed solely within the medical establishment itself, to improve care management in general and such areas as treatment compliance in particular. They also offer a potential that is changing the way healthcare is delivered by helping the system transition away from the traditional series of acute-care interventions to an ongoing focus on health and wellness.

For older adults, the ability to remotely monitor and analyze a range of biologic data offers essential support for being able to age in place within their own homes. It helps reduce costly hospital re-admission rates by keeping track of people who are recently discharged, a particularly vulnerable time for many. And for millions of individuals with chronic conditions, it provides a connection with care providers that has been missing for many people who have fallen through the cracks in the healthcare system.

In all of these cases, tracking physiological parameters through wearable and portable technology is highly effective in identifying potential health risks and catching changes in someone's condition before they become more serious. The result has been, and will continue to be on an even larger scale, improved health outcomes for people taking advantage of the technology, as well as a significant reduction in overall costs for everyone involved.

The familiar physician meets the digital revolution

The adoption of digital technology and its incorporation into existing healthcare procedures constitute the best of both worlds for primary care medicine. PCP practices are well positioned to interpret and then act on the data that's transmitted by a wide range of wearable and portable devices, while also being the first line of defense for patient safety and quality of care. The PCP, especially when he or she is acting in the role of a familiar physician, can also recognize the signs that may indicate a potential change in your health and then develop treatment plans accordingly.

At the same time, with multiple streams of personal health-related information available, your PCP is the best resource for seeing "the big picture" when it comes to your health through her or his ability to turn the data of digital healthcare into knowledge and then translate that knowledge into effective care. In addition, the same kind technology that enables consumers to be more aware of and better informed about their health also connects care providers to evidence-based information that helps them deal with the ever-expanding knowledge base of modern medicine.

It's worth noting that because the digital level of engagement doesn't involve face-to-face encounters between a doctor and patient, basically the only interaction that fee-for-service medicine recognizes, the digital health revolution will also have to include some changes in the way healthcare is paid for and physicians are compensated. Fortunately, those changes are considered in the Affordable Care Act in the form of value-based medicine and are an important component of the Patient-Centered Medical Home.

Maintaining the human touch

It's rarely a safe bet to say "never" in healthcare, but we're going to go out on a limb and say that the vitally important and highly therapeutic bond between a doctor and a patient, which we've discussed a number of times in this book, will never be duplicated by a device or an app, no matter how sophisticated it may be.

What's far more likely is that being freed up from a number of tasks and time commitments that technology can capably handle will let your doctor have even more personalized time with you. Part of this time will be used to coordinate your care more effectively with other care providers on the care team. Another part will be strengthening the human relationship that plays such an essential role in the quality of care. In this way, digital healthcare won't be replacing your familiar physician; it will be extending his or her reach.

SOME EQUAL TIME ON THE SUBJECT OF EQUAL HEALTHCARE

For someone who spent his short life deeply involved in the area of civil rights, Martin Luther King, Jr. managed to touch on a serious healthcare problem with a remark that's as true now as it was when he said it half a century ago: "Of all the forms of inequality, injustice in healthcare is the most shocking and inhumane."

What existed then and what exists now, hopefully to a somewhat lesser degree, is two side-by-side but different healthcare systems. One is for the advantaged—and in this case that includes not just people with major financial assets, but also anyone with higher-end, comprehensive, and private health coverage. The other one is for the disadvantaged, the poor, and uninsured, a group that has a disproportionate representation of people of color, women and children, the disabled, and the working poor.

What it means is that millions of people, and this now includes those whose coverage has seen significant increases in out-of-pocket costs, aren't visiting a physician when they get sick. When they do, they're not getting a recommended test, treatment, or follow-up care. Many of them don't get prescriptions filled, or they may skip doses or take half the prescribed dose in order to save money.

To put it on a very human level, a prominent cardiovascular surgeon, speaking to his colleagues at a professional conference in post-Katrina New Orleans, said, "For the economically disadvantaged, all of our technological sophistication is irrelevant. If you can't afford $50 a month in blood pressure medications, it doesn't matter that we can ablate your atrial arrhythmias using advanced, magnetically-guided robotic catheter placement."

While it won't completely remedy the problem and in fact, creates new problems of its own in the area of high deductibles for some health coverage, the Affordable Care Act's focus on primary care as a way to improve health and lower costs across the total population is a good start. In addition, the strategies now in place for transitioning from fee-for-service to value-based compensation for healthcare providers represent another promising move toward reducing disparity. In the meantime, consider this:

Regardless of your philosophy, ideology, religious affiliation, politics, or personal feelings, relegating a large portion of Americans to substandard healthcare is not a very humane thing to do. But even beyond the humane part of the equation, it doesn't make sense economically. One way or another, whether it's through taxes or through cost shifting—charging more for people who can pay to make up for people who can't—we all pay for the cost of care for the economically disadvantaged. And right now we're not getting our money's worth.

An improved system of delivering and paying for primary care, one that better crosses all socioeconomic lines to provide access to a familiar physician and incentives to help people stay well, will ultimately lead to a stronger economy and a stronger, healthier, and more equitable nation.

Chapter 12:

SHOW ME THE MONEY: PULLING BACK THE CURTAIN ON HEALTHCARE COSTS (AND SAVING A LOT IN THE PROCESS)

REFERRING TO THE FOREIGN policy of the Soviet Union, British statesman Winston Churchill described it as, "A puzzle inside a riddle wrapped in an enigma." Until very recently, if you were a consumer looking to find information about such basic but important areas as quality and price, you might have said the same thing about our healthcare system. The analogy usually given is if you wouldn't buy a car without shopping around, why would you purchase healthcare, something far more critical and usually more expensive, without any comparison of services and costs?

Well, the answer would seem to be there really wasn't much choice. The people who held the keys—the hospitals, physician practices, and insurers—simply weren't opening any doors. And most people didn't mind because they were, as we've described earlier in the chapter on insurance, insulated from the costs.

Along with consumer and governmental pressure for greater transparency, what's changed all that is the noticeable increase in cost sharing related to health coverage. Copays and deductibles have increased considerably for many people, and suddenly getting a better deal (and that can mean anything from saving hundreds to thousands of dollars for the same procedure or service) seems like a really good idea.

WHAT SHOULD BE IN PLACE TO EFFECTIVELY SHOP FOR CARE?

The first and most important requisite is access to information about provider quality, whether it's organizations or individuals. Without that, you're just looking for the best price, and in healthcare as in other fields, that may not be the most important criterion. At the same time, don't confuse high costs with high quality or lower costs with lower quality. There may be no connection. What matters most is having access to credible and unbiased quality measurement tools, and fortunately more and more are becoming available. Then it's a question of balancing cost and quality. After all, that's what value is all about, and healthcare is no exception.

You might also want to consider that some medical situations represent a more appropriate opportunity for comparison shopping than others. For example:

- It helps when the diagnosis has already been made. Otherwise, you're shopping before you know what you need.

- Comparing costs makes more sense for straightforward procedures that don't involve a lot of complexity and don't require much customization to your specific medical needs. That way, there's going to be less concern about clinical quality, and you can focus more on the price.

- It's always less stressful when the anticipated procedure is elective or at the very least not urgent. That one is pretty obvious. You can afford to put a lot of time into shopping for a total knee replacement. A stroke, not so much.

- Shopping also makes more sense economically when the specific provisions of your coverage benefits make looking for lower cost alternatives worth the effort. Generally that means the more stake you have in the process, through copays and high deductibles, the more price shopping makes sense.

FIND THE INFORMATION YOU NEED TO BE A SUCCESSFUL SHOPPER FOR BETTER, LESS EXPENSIVE CARE

The mystery at the heart of healthcare costs, or at least one of them, includes the fact that the people and organizations that provide care have traditionally not publicized what they get paid for their services—unless it involves the perspective that what they get paid isn't enough. The mystery thickens when you consider that what they get paid can vary depending on where the money is coming from. Insurers have been complicit in this arrangement, since they haven't wanted to make it easy to follow the various deals they work out to pay different providers. At the same time, health insurance companies often negotiate with the providers to get lower prices for their covered customers. These amounts rarely see the light of day, either.

When they do, the results can be a startling example of why consumers can't always rely on their health plan's contract to deliver the lowest price, since the same insurer might pay widely varying amounts to different care providers. In an interview with Andrew Webber of the Maine Health Management Coalition, a nonprofit organization based in Topsham, Maine, whose members include health plans, he gave an example of the variation that can exist in costs: One insurer's preferred provider organization (PPO) made payments that ranged between $559 and $4,526 for the same procedure (a colonoscopy) in the same year, according to data compiled by the state.

But as we mentioned, all those smoke and mirrors are going away for the most part. A combination of online resources ranging from payers and government agencies to consumer advocates and the care providers themselves now provides a wealth of comparative and other price information that can help you save hundreds of dollars, even thousands, on a single medical procedure.

At this point, some of the information can be a little confusing, and unlike checking out the price of a particular TV model from a consumer electronics supplier, the healthcare sites don't—and often can't—give exact prices when you're comparing services. At the very least, however, you can get a rough idea.

One of these resources, the Healthcare Bluebook, offers what they call the "Fair Price" for services. The Fair Price represents the reasonable amount you should pay as calculated from a nationwide database of medical payment data and then customized by ZIP code to your specific area. Because many medical procedures, hip replacements being a good example, have multiple components, the Fair Price includes a number or range for the services of the surgeon performing the procedure; the cost of hospital services including overnight stays, nursing, supplies, and most medications; and the services of the anesthesiologist which are typically billed separately.

The resources below are available to everyone and provide the kind of information that can help you be a more informed healthcare shopper. Note that health insurers also have comparative data on services, but it's only available to the people covered by that particular plan:

Castlight Health: castlighthealth.com
Centers for Medicare and Medicaid Services: cms.gov (go. cms.gov/1IQCgSR)
Change Healthcare: changehealthcare.com
Healthcare Bluebook: healthcarebluebook.com
SpendWell: spendwellhealth.com
Symbiosis Health: symbiosishealth.com
Medicare's site: Hospital.Compare.hhs.gov

MORE WAYS TO SAVE MONEY: CHALLENGE UNREASONABLE BILLS

It's always best to get as much information as you can *before* you actually receive healthcare services and to have a reasonable sense of what to expect. Sometimes it doesn't work that way, though, and your advocating efforts on behalf of yourself or a family member or friend begin with the bill—or more likely bills—when it comes in. If that happens, keep these two points in mind:

First, Medical Billing Advocates of America, a Roanoke, Virginia-based firm specializing in research and education related to medical billing and insurance company payments, estimates that up to 80% of hospital bills contain errors. Most of these mistakes appear to be unintentional and are based on coding errors (understandable, given the amount of separate data entry sources that go into billing), but unacceptable nonetheless.

Second, the other thing to consider is the way that hospitals levy charges. Hospital "chargemasters," a comprehensive list of items that are billable to a patient or insurance provider, represent the care providers "sticker price." In other words, the chargemaster usually contains highly inflated prices and should be considered as a starting point only for negotiations rather than an absolute and unmovable set of costs. At any point in the process, here are some tips that can be helpful in dealing with high bills:

Ask for an itemized bill

Patients typically receive a summary bill that provides only a fraction of the detail for the charges being billed. Never pay the summarized amount, even if requested to do so at the time of discharge. Contact the business office and immediately ask for an itemized bill.

Request an audit of your bill

Ask for an audit when charges appear excessive or when you spot duplicate charges or line items for services you can't recall receiving. Hospitals will then generally assign a staff member to review your bill charge by charge.

Ask for a cost reduction

Contact the hospital or surgeon's billing office to ask for a cost reduction. It's a practice that at the very least will communicate that you find the bill excessive. You'll never know if you don't ask, so request that the billing office charge you what an insurance company would realistically pay the hospital for that same service. In this instance, as in all transactions related to billing, it helps to do your homework (see the resources we listed for comparative pricing) and negotiate from an informed position.

Negotiate a realistic monthly payment

The billing source will probably suggest a monthly payment, with terms that will enable you to pay a little every month and avoid collection action. Always ask for an amount you think you can pay without bringing undue financial burdens on you and your family.

Hire a medical bill negotiation service

Hospital bills and their multiple components are often confusing. For some people, hiring an advocate or negotiation service can be a good way to go. These professionals are familiar with medical codes and use a database with hospital-specific and procedure-specific information that documents reasonable charges. Most of these individuals or services charge either an hourly fee or a percentage (typically up to 35% of the amount they save you). Nonprofit organizations sometimes offer similar services free of charge.

Appeal insurance claim denials

This isn't quite the same as dealing with a hospital bill, but it's definitely something that will affect the cost of your care. The first thing to know is that you should never assume a denied claim is the final answer. Many denials are based on incomplete or inaccurate information, a question of eligibility, or maybe even a technical error in the billing code. In fact, only about half of health insurance claims denials are based on a disagreement over the medical appropriateness of the care.

If that's the case (and your insurer is required to tell you why your claim was denied as well as how to appeal it), get your doctor on board. He or she may need to write a "letter of medical necessity." In all cases, you have a reasonably good chance (usually estimated to be at least 50-50) of getting the decision changed.

The resolution may not be easy, and it may involve what

seems like endless hours on the phone, but you have a legal right to appeal any decision—with the knowledge that insurance companies are likely hoping you won't go through the process. Along with your doctor, you can also turn to a social worker at the hospital (assuming the denied claim is related to hospital-based services) for help in navigating an often-complex system.

A FEW WORDS ABOUT PRESCRIPTION DRUGS

If you're having problems related to the cost of prescription medications, be aware that there are assistance programs that provide free or low-cost prescriptions to those who meet income-eligibility guidelines. Some of the patient assistance programs (PAPs) are operated by state government agencies, but most are run by pharmaceutical companies, which means you'll get their brand name drugs.

Beyond that, the many online purchases that people make and the discount at several big-box retail stores and pharmacies, there really is no magic formula for saving on prescription meds. And the whole process can be complicated by the fact that insurance companies often change their formularies—the list of prescription drugs covered by your plan—over the course of a year or several years.

You can refer to the directories in the back of this book for assistance program details and other cost-saving tips for getting your prescriptions at lower cost.

AND SOME FINAL WORDS ABOUT SAVING MONEY

For just about as long as doctors and hospitals have been billing people for services, and as long as health insurers have been in the business of providing coverage, we've been led to believe that we don't have any control over costs. Now through increased transparency all around and the availability of a growing range of tools and resources, you can change that old paradigm.

Think of it like this. Lowering healthcare costs is one of the most important priorities we have as a nation and a driving force behind every healthcare initiative. There's no reason why those lowered costs can't begin with you.

Chapter 13:

A PREVIEW OF HEALTHCARE'S FUTURE

OVER THE COURSE OF this book we've looked at a number of the dramatic changes being made throughout the field of healthcare. These innovations are transforming the way your doctor and your care team do their jobs. Equally important, the changes are putting you even more securely at the center of your care.

Given the developments that are driving healthcare in our present time, you can't help wondering what the future holds. In our estimation, it gets even better.

Using the analogy of the national efforts and accomplishments put forth in the 1960s quest to "land a man on the moon and return him safely to earth," we are roughly at the stage NASA was at when a space capsule orbiting the Earth several times was rightfully considered a landmark achievement. It won't be long, however, until we have achieved the healthcare equivalent of humans landing on the moon, or to update the analogy a bit, having unmanned vehicles take close-up photos of Pluto.

The "moon shot" mission in healthcare now is to use leading-edge technology not only to save lives and increase the quality of life for countless people, but also to strengthen the healing relationship of trust between physicians and patients. Toward that objective, picture this scenario:

You wake up one day feeling pain in your abdomen. This isn't ordinary pain that goes away in a short time, so you decide you need to see your primary care physician.

You make an appointment online, and a short time later you're in front of your doctor. No one has taken your temperature or blood pressure—that information was already captured at home by your inexpensive wearable device or from an app on your smart phone. The doctor doesn't ask you where it hurts—you already provided that information when you made the online appointment.

Instead of all those preliminaries, the doctor gets right to it. She or he goes to the computer and examines a list of possible diagnoses that have already been accessed, ranked by most likely to least likely. Those diagnoses are not copied from a general list of diagnoses for "abdominal pain," but instead are careful calculations based on an exceptionally in-depth analysis of your personal information—your vital signs, your medical history as well as the medical histories of thousands of other people with the same complaint, your genetic makeup, and a review of all the medical studies on the subject of abdominal pain. With this incredibly rich and personalized information readily available, your doctor uses his or her own knowledge to evaluate all of the options being presented, and the recommended treatments, to determine the best course of action.

All of this happens in minutes, sometimes even seconds. The rest of your appointment is then spent in conversation with your doctor to help the two of you work together to develop a plan of care that not only addresses your immediate pain, but is designed to prevent the same problem from occurring in the future. The plan of care is based on your input of what you can (and are willing) to do. It takes into account your work schedule, family life, financial status, transportation needs, and social situation. Most important of all, it reflects your goals. In other words, your care plan is built to serve you through your own highly personalized input. And as a personal and societal bonus, the entire encounter is designed to minimize the cost of care from start to finish.

If that all seems just a bit different that your own personal experiences in a doctor's exam room these days, consider that quite a few people were shaking their heads when President Kennedy talked about walking on the moon half a century ago. But the fact is, this futuristic-sounding medical encounter is achievable today and will be part of your experience as long as we remain committed, both as individuals and as a nation, to improving our healthcare system.

COMPUTERS THAT THINK

As good as today's population health management technology is, it promises to get even better in the very near future thanks to such advancements in "cognitive computing" as IBM's Watson platform. Before looking at more information on cognitive computing, which basically means computer systems modeled more closely after the human brain, let's briefly examine how limitations in today's computers diminish their ability to help physicians deliver better care.

One of the challenges physicians face in delivering the best possible level of care is the high volume of "unstructured" or freeform data that exists on their patients. This is information that health providers type into the "notes" section in a patient's electronic health record rather than into a specific field in the software. Since most computers are programmed to look only for data in these structured fields, the unstructured notes get lost.

Unfortunately, the notes section of the digital chart is where most providers find it easiest to record important insights about a patient's condition. If the computer can't read them, it's as if the notes don't exist. So a critical part of your medical history may not be visible when data is being gathered. Other examples of unstructured data include lab and radiology results (such as X-rays and MRIs).

As you can imagine, that represents some critical information that isn't coming into play. And it's part of the reason why an estimated one-third of all diagnoses by medical professionals are incorrect or incomplete. That doesn't remotely mean that one-third of doctors are incompetent or that they aren't thorough one-third of the time. What it means is that it's far too easy for them to miss important data, especially if it is unstructured information like notes.

IBM invented cognitive computing to solve this problem. Cognitive computing systems not only can "see" unstructured data, but also interpret it the way a human would. They can evaluate what is important to the task at hand and what should be ignored in delivering a diagnosis and the best treatment recommendations. Just as important, cognitive computing systems can learn from their successes and their errors, just as we humans do. Only they learn millions of times faster. This makes cognitive computing one of the single most powerful tools we have to improve the practice of medicine.

In a discussion on the power of cognitive computing with Dr. Mark Kris, a medical oncologist at Memorial Sloane Kettering Cancer Center in New York, we learned about the capabilities of this technology in very real terms. Dr. Kris explained that one of his patients had 286 pages of unstructured digitized data in his records, and it took one of his staff a full week to sort through all of it to uncover the most important information. The same data was fed into IBM Watson—a cognitive computing system made famous when it defeated a Jeopardy champion on live TV—and Watson immediately revealed the unstructured data in a dropdown menu on the computer screen. Watson also recognized and highlighted the most important information to assure it wasn't missed.

Dr. Kris then asked Watson for the most likely diagnosis and course of treatment for his patient. In less than a second, the computer searched the world's medical libraries for information about the patient's particular type of lung cancer, matched it against his genomic profile, medical history, and the medical histories of other people with the same type of condition. Watson then provided the top five most likely diagnoses for the patient, assigning each one a probability. The top diagnosis, which had a probability of 98%, was based on a paper that had been published just one week before in an obscure Israeli medical journal that Dr. Kris said he was unlikely to have ever read on his own.

The example illustrates another important advantage that cognitive computers have in helping physicians deliver better care—their immensely greater capacity for storing knowledge. Even the best human minds have a limited capacity to absorb information. It's been estimated that the volume of information in healthcare journals, research studies, and clinical trials doubles every five years. Keeping up with all of that information is like trying to drink from a fire hose. In fact, based on that volume, the typical physician is roughly 500–1,000 years behind in his or her reading.

It's clear that the 20th century model of training physicians, where we take the best and brightest students and use their minds as knowledge repositories, is no longer viable. Using manual computer search engines fares little better, because the physician must guess the right keyword terms to search on; if an important document doesn't fit the keywords, it could be missed.

Computers, however, are designed for that very purpose— to absorb, dissect, and store massive volumes of information. Cognitive computing takes it to the next step, enabling the computer to make decisions on how information is presented in order to provide physicians with the highest-probability solutions first—and to learn from their successes and failures as physicians record whether or not the diagnosis or treatment was right.

Among its other advantages, this type of system becomes a critical error-prevention tool. An estimated 100,000 Americans die each year from medical errors. Cognitive computing can cut your chances of being exposed to a life-threatening medical error in half. No one could disagree on that particular capability being an extremely gratifying development for both healthcare providers and their patients.

OWNING YOUR OWN MEDICAL RECORDS

One other important change for the future will be who owns your medical records. Just as you will become the centerpiece of your care, in the future you will also become the owner of your medical records, a major step in what some people call the "democratization" of medicine.

Let's go back to our original scenario, where you contact your physician about abdominal pain. Only this time, you're halfway across the country when the pain occurs. If you go to the emergency department at the local hospital today, they have no idea what your medical history is or what prescriptions you're currently taking unless you tell them. Those records are locked up in the EHRs of your providers.

In the future, though, you will have direct access to all your records through a patient portal. If you are out of town, or decide to visit a specialist who is not in a network with your primary care physician, you can simply log in to the portal, and your entire history becomes available to the provider in front of you at the point of care. All of that information then becomes available to help you work with that physician to create a plan of care that fits you specifically.

A FUTURE THAT WILL BENEFIT ALL OF US

You're part of the early stages of building a new system of care that includes a healing relationship of trust between you and the providers you use. Under the medical home model we talked about earlier, your primary care physician will help you manage your care, acting as a coach rather than a quarterback, and linking to other care providers in a network that is often called a "medical neighborhood" in which the medical home is an essential part. Those providers will be accountable for getting your care right the first time, and with the physician payment reforms we also talked about earlier, will have a financial incentive to ensure you get healthy and stay that way.

To support that goal, your providers (and you) will have instant access to the accumulated medical knowledge of the world, already parsed and prioritized and delivered in an easily digestible form at the point of care, along with a broad range of data about you personally as well as the people with whom you share similarities. This information will be used to help support your physician's decisions, reducing medical errors, lowering costs, and delivering better outcomes.

All of this future isn't here quite yet, but it's coming, and like you, we're very much looking forward to its arrival.

Afterword

SOME FINAL THOUGHTS BEFORE WE GO

Our message and our time with you have come to an end, but your journey through the ever-changing world of healthcare continues. As you navigate forward, one very important factor in your favor is that you're living in a remarkable convergence of ages. The Age of the Internet has morphed seamlessly with the Age of Social Media. Together they've helped create the Age of the Consumer, a time when access to both extensive information and a wealth (at times, it might seem like an overload) of commentary about that information is unprecedented.

What that means for consumers of healthcare, which all of us are or will be, is that there's no better time to be well informed and confident about the decisions we make regarding care, from finding a familiar physician, scheduling an appointment, and learning more about a diagnosis to comparing quality and price across multiple sources.

For the first time in the history of modern medicine, innovations in information technology are going to influence healthcare as much, or perhaps even more, than innovations in conventional medical technology. If you're tech savvy, that's going to help. If not, there's a good chance you'll be able to get assistance from people who are. Either way, it's your time, so find the best way to take advantage of it.

Our sincere hope is that what we've provided in this book—those threads of information about medical homes, familiar physicians, new approaches to primary care, engaging with your providers, and cost-saving tools—help form a tapestry of personal health that stays with you and your family for years to come.

—Dr. Peter Anderson and Dr. Paul Grundy

About the Authors

PETER B. ANDERSON, MD

Dr. Anderson completed his MD at the University of Virginia School of Medicine and his residency training at Riverside Regional Medical Center in Newport News, Virginia. He maintained a large primary care practice for 30 years, which became the first in the state of Virginia to be recognized and accredited by the National Committee for Quality Assurance (NCQA) as a medical home. While in practice, Dr. Anderson also served as Clinical Assistant Professor of Family Medicine at the University of Virginia School of Medicine and Assistant Professor of Clinical Family and Community Medicine at Eastern Virginia Medical School.

After retiring from active practice, he founded and now leads Team Care Medicine™, a healthcare consulting and training company. Using a model of inside-the-exam-room care that serves to both redesign traditional workflow patterns and elevate staff responsibilities, Dr. Anderson has helped over 300 physician practices, as well as U.S. Department of Defense Military Health primary care clinics, transform their practices.

The author of three books, including *The Familiar Physician* which focuses on the patient-physician bond and the

Patient-Centered Medical Home as key elements of primary care medicine and health reform, Dr. Anderson is also a frequent national speaker and media contributor on family practice and primary care issues.

To learn more about Dr. Anderson and his work, visit teamcaremedicine.com or follow @thefamiliarphys on Twitter.

"I spent several days with Dr. Anderson and his team to see this innovative practice style firsthand. I quickly became convinced that this was how primary care, and primary care physicians, could survive...."

—Kevin Hopkins, MD
Cleveland Clinic Family Practice Management

PAUL H. GRUNDY, MD

Paul Grundy, MD, MPH, FACOEM, FACPM, currently serves as IBM's Global Director of Healthcare Transformation and is a member of the IBM Industry Academy. He attended medical school at the University of California, San Francisco, completed his residency training in Preventive Medicine and a postdoctoral fellowship in Occupational Health in the International Environment, both at Johns Hopkins. Dr. Grundy also earned a Master's Degree in Public Health at the University of California, Berkeley.

He is a member of the National Academy of Science's Institute of Medicine, Chair of Health Policy for the Employee Retirement Income Security Act (ERISA), and an adjunct professor at the University of Utah Department of Family and Preventive Medicine. In 2014, Dr. Grundy was named as Ambassador for Healthcare DENMARK, a role in which he shares best practices from the Danish healthcare system with U.S. and international physicians.

Prior to his career at IBM, Dr. Grundy was a medical officer and flight surgeon in the U.S. Air Force and served in the U.S. Department of State, where he advised ambassadors on healthcare programs for diplomatic posts. He received the

Department of State Superior Honor Award for efforts related to the HIV/AIDS crisis in sub-Saharan Africa.

Dr. Grundy also served as Chief Medical Office for the Adventist Health System, Pennsylvania, and is currently president of the Patient-Centered Care Collaborative, a not-for-profit advocacy group committed to advancing an effective health system built on a strong foundation of primary care and the Patient-Centered Medical Home. Dr. Grundy is widely known as "the Godfather of the medical home."

You can follow Dr. Grundy on Twitter at @Paul_PCPCC.

"Dr. Paul Grundy may be the most knowledgeable person in the United States regarding the state of our country's healthcare."

—Craig Jones, MD,
Executive Director, Vermont Blueprint for Health

TOM EMSWILLER

Tom Emswiller is a freelance writer living in San Jose, California. As a copywriter at Young & Rubicam Company and later as creative director at Medimetrix Group, his work focused on healthcare education, communications, and policy dissemination. He also worked extensively with the Robert Wood Johnson Foundation's Communities in Charge program, an initiative developed to promote preventive care and improve healthcare delivery for the uninsured. Mr. Emswiller graduated from Duke University, holds an advanced degree in journalism from Boston University, and is a former VISTA volunteer.

BUD RAMEY

Bud Ramey completed a long career in health system marketing, communications, and public affairs and has co-authored five nonfiction books on a range of healthcare and social issues.

He has received numerous national awards for excellence in communications and humanitarian and community collaboration, including the *Foster McGaw Prize* from the American Hospital Association. He also received the Public Affairs *Silver Anvil Award* from the Public Relations Society of America, the industry's most distinguished honor. Mr. Ramey lives in coastal Virginia and is a graduate of the Virginia Military Institute.

Bibliography

AAP Medical Home Model. (n.d.). Retrieved August 28, 2015, from http://digitalnavigator.aap.org/Pages/AAP-Medical-Home-Model.aspx

Adams, D. (1980). *The Hitchhiker's Guide to the Galaxy*. New York: Harmony Books.

Gawande, A. (2014). *Being mortal: Medicine and what matters in the end.* Metropolitan Books.

Makary, M. (2013). *Unaccountable: What hospitals won't tell you and how transparency can revolutionize health care.* New York: Bloomsbury Press.

APPENDIX

Glossary of Terms

Acute care: an immediate medical need requiring treatment.

Accountable Care Organization (ACO): a healthcare organization characterized by a group of healthcare providers contracted together to be responsible for the health, the healthcare, and the cost of healthcare for an assigned population of patients.

Affordable Care Act (ACA): The Patient Protection and Affordable Care Act (PPACA), called the Affordable Care Act (ACA) or Obamacare, is a United States federal statute signed into law by President Barack Obama on March 23, 2010.

Allowed amount: the maximum amount (also called "eligible expense," "negotiated rate," and "payment allowance") your insurance plan will cover for a specific healthcare service. You may have to pay the difference if you see a provider who charges more than the allowed amount. (See "Balance billing.")

Balance billing: when an out-of-network provider bills you for the remaining balance after your insurance pays its allowed amount for non-network providers. You won't encounter balance billing with a preferred (in-network) provider because he or she provides services as part of the insurance network agreement.

Benefits: healthcare services that are covered under your insurance plan.

Benefit exclusions: a healthcare product or service that is not considered eligible for coverage (payment) by a health insurance plan.

Catastrophic plan: minimal insurance support until a very high deductible is met. The premium amount you pay each month for healthcare is generally lower, but the out-of-pocket costs for deductibles, copayments, and coinsurance are higher.

Chronic care management: routine follow-up to manage long-term illness.

Coinsurance: your share of the costs for a specific covered service. This amount is calculated as a percentage (e.g., 30%) of the amount your plan allows for the service. You pay the coinsurance amount and any deductible you owe, and your plan covers the rest of the allowed amount for the service.

Concierge medicine: a direct contract between you and your doctor for you to receive medical services in a more personal and timely fashion.

Copayment: fixed amount (e.g., $20, $30, $50) you pay when you receive services covered by your health plan (usually paid at the time services are rendered). The copay amount varies by your plan and the type of service you receive.

Cost sharing: the share of costs of benefits that you pay out-of-pocket. This generally includes deductibles, coinsurance, copayments, or similar charges but doesn't include premiums, the cost of non-covered services, or balance billing for non-network providers. Individuals with low income who are buying insurance plans from the Health Insurance Marketplace may qualify for cost-sharing financial assistance.

Deductible: the amount you pay out-of-pocket for covered services before your insurance pays the balance.

Diagnostic care: intervention sought for symptoms or complications of an illness. These tests are necessary for managing illness and not considered preventive care, so coinsurance rules apply (in contrast to preventive tests, which are free).

Direct Primary Care: a form of Concierge Medicine that balances a heavier patient load (heavier than Concierge Medicine but still much lighter than a conventional practice) on the part of the doctor with lower monthly fees.

Familiar physician: a physician who you know and trust and who knows you.

Fee-for-Service (FFS): payment structure in which health care providers are paid for each service they render (an office visit, test, procedure, etc.).

Health Insurance Marketplace: government resource where individuals, families, and small business can find and enroll in a plan. Also called the exchange.

HMO: a type of managed care plan in which you can only go to doctors, other healthcare providers, or hospitals on the plan's list except in an emergency. To see a specialist, you need to get a referral from your primary care doctor. You generally must get your care and services from doctors, other healthcare providers, or hospitals in the plan's network.

Health plan: a specific insurance company contracted with a specific network with a set of rules that govern the care inside and outside the network.

Insurance plan: a specific insurance company contracted with a specific network with a set of rules that govern the care inside and outside the network.

Managed care: a contractual agreement between an insurance company and a network designed to improve quality and lower costs. This agreement places restrictions (rules) on providers available to the participants.

Medicaid: the Health Insurance Association of America describes Medicaid as a "government insurance program for persons of all ages whose income and resources are insufficient to pay for health care."

Medicare: a national insurance program, administered by the federal government since 1966, that provides health insurance for Americans aged 65 and older who have worked and paid into the system. It also provides health insurance to younger people with certain disabilities.

Network: a group of healthcare providers.

Non-covered services: a benefit exclusion of the plan or the result of not obtaining prior authorization before receiving a service.

Out-of-network: when a member uses a hospital, physician, or other providers that do not have a contract with the insurance plan.

Out-of-pocket costs: your expenses for health services that aren't reimbursed by your insurance plan. These include deductibles, copayments, and coinsurance for covered services and the costs of all non-covered services.

Out-of-pocket maximum/limit: the most you'll have to pay during a policy year before your plan starts to cover 100% of the costs for essential benefits. This amount includes deductibles, coinsurance, copayments, or any other costs for medically necessary care covered by your plan. It doesn't include premiums, out-of-network costs, or the costs of non-covered services. Once you reach your plan's maximum, you won't have any more out-of-pocket expenses for the rest of the policy year.

Patient-Centered Medical Home (PCMH): a new approach to primary care that relies on accessible, comprehensive, and coordinated care delivered through a high-performing team. It has become a widely accepted model for how primary care should be organized and delivered throughout the healthcare system.

Patient-Centered Primary Care Collaborative (PCPCC): The PCPCC describes themselves as "a not-for-profit membership organization dedicated to advancing an effective and efficient health system built on a strong foundation of primary care and the Patient-Centered Medical Home."

Payers: an insurance company, employer, or government – the main entities that pay for healthcare services.

Prior authorization: a requirement that their members receive approval before undergoing specific medical treatments, tests, or surgical procedures.

POS: A point-of-service plan (POS) is a type of managed care plan that is a hybrid of HMO and PPO plans. Like an HMO, participants designate an in-network physician to be their primary care provider. But like a PPO, patients may go outside of the provider network for healthcare services. You pay less with a POS plan if you stay within the plan's network. You're also required to obtain a referral from your primary care doctor before seeing a specialist.

PPO: A preferred provider organization (or PPO) is a type of managed care plan with more freedom to see providers inside the network and outside the network. You pay less if you use the providers within a PPO network, but you can go outside the network without a referral (for an additional cost). PPOs are the most expensive insurance plan because of the large network size and (usually) good out-of-network coverage.

Premium: the annual amount you pay for your insurance plan's covered benefits (usually paid in monthly installments). The higher the monthly payments, the lower the out-of-pocket costs for services received during the year.

Preventive care/services: routine care (when you're symptom-free) such as physical exams, recommended screenings, and patient education/counseling to prevent illness or disease. This care is fully covered by insurance as long as it was obtained after the ACA went into effect.

Primary care physician (PCP, comprehensivist): the Institute of Medicine defines primary care as "the provision of integrated accessible healthcare services by clinicians who are accountable for addressing a large majority of personal healthcare needs, developing a sustained partnership with patients, and practicing in the context of family and community."

Providers: healthcare providers include hospitals, doctors, nurse practitioners, physician assistants, pharmacies, nursing homes, physical therapy, etc. – any entity that provides a covered healthcare benefit.

Price transparency: readily available information on the price of healthcare services to help define the value of those services and enable purchasers to identify, compare, and choose providers that offer the desired level of value.

Resources of Special Interest to the Uninsured and Underinsured

Despite the dramatic increase in individuals with health insurance—the largest since Medicare and Medicaid were introduced over 50 years ago—made possible through the Affordable Care Act, many Americans still lack basic health coverage. This situation is especially prevalent in those states that have opted out of Medicaid expansion.

At the same time, there are millions of people who have some level of health insurance, but lack the scope of coverage or the affordable access needed to meet a number of essential healthcare needs. Most of these individuals have entered the ranks of the underinsured because of financial reasons. If you or someone you know is part of either group, or if you want to know more about what help is available, the information that follows will be of significant value.

This information, in the form of two comprehensive directories for the uninsured and underinsured respectively is reprinted in *Lost and Found* with the kind permission of the Patient Advocate Foundation, a nonprofit organization with headquarters in Hampton, Virginia. The Patient Advocate

Foundation developed these directories and is solely responsible for their content. Because of their relevance to healthcare in general as well as their relationship to the consumer information we have provided to help you navigate the healthcare system, we are presenting the directories in their entirety. While the directories duplicate some of the descriptions of services, glossary items, and specific resources you've already read about in *Lost and Found*, this is useful and valuable information that warrants a little repetition.

We're grateful to the Patient Advocate Foundation for their generosity in sharing this important resource and encourage you to use the contact information within the directories for any questions you may have.

The Patient Advocate Foundation
National Underinsured Resource Directory
National Uninsured Resource Directory

HELP WITH HEALTHCARE PROBLEMS

Patient Advocate Foundation (PAF), a nonprofit with a four-star rating from Charity Navigator, provides patients with arbitration, mediation, and negotiation to settle issues with access to care, medical debt, and job retention related to their illness.

Patient Advocate Foundation
421 Butler Farm Road, Hampton, Virginia 23666
1-800-532-5274 / 1-757-873-6668 | patientadvocate.org

CO-PAY RELIEF FOR INSURED PATIENTS

The Foundation's Co-Pay Relief Program provides direct financial assistance to insured patients who meet certain qualifications to help them pay for the prescriptions and/or treatments they need. This assistance helps patients afford the out-of-pocket costs for these items that their insurance companies require.

This program offers many online tools for patients, providers, and pharmacy representatives, including 24-hour web-based portals, electronic signature, document upload, and bar code fax routing capabilities.

Co-Pay Relief's patient assistance, purely donor-funded, disperses money to qualified patients, while funds are available for each disease.

1-888-512-3861 / Option 1 | copays.org

Erin Singleton

Chief of Mission Delivery, Patient Advocate Foundation

Erin Singleton has been a long-standing member of the Foundation for most of its nearly 20-year history, previously serving as Senior Case Manager, Quality Assurance Officer, and Chief of External Communications, working with catastrophically ill individuals to educate, empower, and proactively assist them. Currently, as Chief of Mission Delivery, Erin oversees the case management and financial aid fund divisions and the organization's communications and data realms and works to ensure every patient has access to free assistance to help overcome barriers in healthcare.

As the Patient Advocate Foundation approaches its 20th year in 2016, it nears the 1,000,000th patient mark in service to those in need.

"I've had the joy of helping to take the dream of Nancy Davenport-Ennis, our founder, and turn it into a mission, and then help expand it," Erin says.

"A lot of people get sick and then find out what their benefits are. Medical debt builds. Collection calls start. Payment plans stress the family budget. They call us to help, and we do," she describes.

"We help those who are diagnosed with serious and chronic conditions who have hit a barrier in their healthcare, including providing insurance support and mediation. In our case management division alone, over half of our patients make under $23,000 a year, creating a very vulnerable population."

Working within case management for years, Erin is very familiar with access to care issues, employment retention, debt crisis, and health insurance issues, as well as community, state, and government resources throughout the United States.

In addition to case management support, Patient Advocate Foundation's Co-Pay Relief Program provides deeply needed support to insured chronically ill patients who struggle to afford their medications. If you qualify, the program can even look back and reimburse you for six months of co-payment expenditures spent on medications.

Throughout her career in patient advocacy, Erin's expertise has been repeatedly sought by national and local media outlets for articles addressing the myriad of practical issues confronting patients reflecting the value of case management. Articles have appeared in numerous media outlets, including: *The Wall Street Journal*, Associated Press, *The New York Times*, *US News and World Report*, *USA Today*, *The Washington Post* and many others.

Erin and her staff developed two key patient-focused publications to help those who are uninsured and those who are underinsured better navigate and prevent insurance hurdles when possible. The Foundation shares guidance from both publications in *Lost and Found*.

Find the Missing Pieces:

NATIONAL UNDERINSURED RESOURCE DIRECTORY OF THE PATIENT ADVOCATE FOUNDATION

Acknowledgment

The National Underinsured Resource Directory has been prepared by the Patient Advocate Foundation (PAF), a leading direct patient services organization in the country with a mission to eliminate obstacles for patients trying to access quality healthcare. PAF seeks to safeguard patients through effective mediation, assuring access to care, maintenance of employment, and preservation of their financial stability relative to their diagnosis of life-threatening or debilitating diseases.

Established in 2008, the Patient Action Council is a forum comprised of like-minded pharmaceutical and biotechnology advocacy executives who seek to provide valuable tools to patients and improve healthcare in the United States.

It is the intention of the Patient Action Council and the Patient Advocate Foundation that this publication be an educational tool to inform uninsured consumers of their options and to provide tips on navigating the healthcare system.

Support for this guide came from Patient Action Council Members:

Amgen Inc.
Eli Lilly and Company
Novartis Pharmaceuticals Corporation
Pfizer Inc.
Sanofi Aventis U.S.

For those with access to the internet, this publication and a comprehensive resource search and interactive tool can be found at patientadvocate.org/underinsured.

Introduction

Beginning in 2008, PAF noted a growing trend within its Patient Data Analysis Report, the annual statistical report compiled from the records of families who were served by PAF's patient service division. Of the patients who contacted PAF, more than 60% reported debt crisis issues as their primary concern. Further research revealed that 56% of those were related to healthcare expenses incurred by a person after the onset of an illness. *We found that nearly 94% of these patients were fully insured.* This last statistic is important, as it reflects a growing crisis among America's underinsured population. These individuals are most frequently working, middle class Americans who are covered by a health insurance plan, but cannot sustain financial stability after they have been diagnosed with a serious illness.

Section 1: Health Insurance and the Underinsured

Even before the new healthcare reform passage, an estimated 25 million Americans were reported to be underinsured. Many people are finding that they are faced with obstacles associated with high medical costs despite having some sort of medical coverage, especially with a new wave of deductibles and co-pays. These people are underinsured.

Health insurance comes in many forms:

- Exchange plans
- Employer-sponsored plans
- Individual/privately purchased plans
- Health Savings Accounts/High-Deductible Health Plans
- Catastrophic/limited benefit plans
- Military/TRICARE
- Medicare Entitlements
- Medicaid Entitlements

When a patient is diagnosed with an illness, he or she may quickly learn that their insurance coverage is inadequate and they are "underinsured." For this publication, underinsured is defined as having some insurance coverage but not enough, or when one is insured yet unable to afford the out-of-pocket responsibilities not covered by his or her insurer. Insurance issues faced by consumers can go full circle, from benefit exclusions to running out of a specific benefit.

We will be discussing issues commonly reported to Patient Advocate Foundation, including a brief definition of each term in the back of the publication. Following the terms, recommendations will be made to help find a positive outcome on your issues. In order to help you navigate the healthcare system, we will divide the issues into two groups: financial and access to care. While you may be impacted by both, we will try to give specific recommendations to help overcome each of these obstacles.

Section 2: Financial Issues

Financial issues often are a result of:

- Inability to afford out-of-pocket costs
- Higher out-of pocket expenses related to out-of-network care
- Pharmacy or medication-related issues
- Inability to afford health insurance premiums (including COBRA)

There are actions to consider if you are having difficulty affording your out-of-pocket responsibilities. Your goal is to find a positive resolution to your issue. These suggestions may help you achieve success.

- Make sure you are getting all the health insurance benefits you are entitled to by reading and following the specific requirements of your health insurance plan. Be sure to pay attention to what services are covered as well as excluded under the definition portion of your plan.

- Review your plan language for a complete list of participating providers and facilities to avoid additional expenses often associated with out-of-network care.

- Seek coverage options through personal or alternatively sponsored plans for better coverage (example employer or spousal coverage).

- Apply for Medicaid programs if you meet the eligibility criteria. In the event you are determined not to be eligible for regular Medicaid, you may be able to qualify for other programs available through Medicaid, such as Qualified Medicare Beneficiaries (QMB), Specified Low-Income Medicare Beneficiary program (SLMB), or a Medicaid Spend-down (you pay a share of cost). You can obtain information on these programs and how to apply by contacting your local Medicaid office.

- Apply for county medical assistance programs when denied Medicaid. This program is not available everywhere. However, when available, the program is a coordinated system for the low-income, uninsured of the county of residence to access needed medical care on a sliding payment scale or at no cost. Contact your local Medicaid office to learn more.

- Seek financial assistance through state, national, or disease-specific co-pay assistance programs listed under the resource section of this book. In addition to the information above, if the issues for which you are seeking assistance involve co-payments, co-insurance, or deductibles, you may want to try the following action step: inquire through hospitals, facilities, or providers about available assistance programs such as prompt-pay discounts, self-pay discounts, partial and full-charity care, or reasonable payment arrangements.

Consider the following when you are approaching or have exceeded an annual, lifetime, or specific cap as outlined in your health insurance plan:

- Inquire through hospitals, facilities, or providers about available assistance programs such as prompt-pay discounts, self-pay discounts, partial and full-charity care, or reasonable payment arrangements.

- Search for a clinical trial that is specific to your diagnosis. Clinical trials are a way for those to access other therapy after they have exhausted traditional or standard care. Clinical trials also provide an avenue to care for the uninsured or underinsured. Some trials absorb most or all of the treatment cost and can be a cost-effective way to access care. The National Institute of Health (NIH) and National Cancer Institute (NCI) offer a broad range of clinical trials. NIH offers a broad range of trials, whereas NCI only offers cancer-related trials. In order to be prescreened for these trials, you must call NCI at 1-888-624-1937 and NIH at 1-800-411-1222 to determine if you fit their criteria.

- EmergingMed offers a free online tool that helps cancer patients find appropriate clinical trials. They may be contacted at 1-877-601-8601 or on their website at emergingmed.com.

- Seek care through community health facilities, free clinics, and your local health department.

You may find the following action steps helpful when you are seeking assistance with pharmacy or medication-related issues:

- Explore discount drug options through large retailers, supermarket, or pharmacy chains such as Walgreens, Wal-Mart, CVS, or Target. Contact your closest retailer to see if a comparable program exists.

- Consider generic-equivalent medications with your doctor's approval.

- Explore mail order options offered by your health insurance plan.

- Check with your provider to see if he or she can offer you samples of the medication.

- Apply for national or disease-specific co-pay assistance programs. There are also free or low-cost drug programs. A complete listing is available in the resource section of this publication.

- Apply for state drug assistance programs by contacting your local state insurance commissioner's office. You can find a link to state specific programs at needymeds.com.

- Drug replacement programs may be available to assist you by providing medications directly to your physician's office for your use. Discuss these programs with your physician. Medicare Part D beneficiaries can call RxAssist at 1-401-729-3284 or visit rxassist.org for a comprehensive database of patient assistance programs.

- Medicare beneficiaries can apply for a low-income subsidy (LIS), also known as Extra Help, to help cover full or partial costs of Medicare Part D. Additional information and eligibility requirements are available on the Social Security Administration website (socialsecurity.gov) or by calling 1-800-772-1213.

Section 3: Access

Even if you have health insurance, there may be times that you find yourself having problems being able to access necessary treatments or procedures due to your insurance plan denying coverage. In this section we will be discussing access to care issues, which you may be experiencing as a result of the following:

- Capped benefits
- Excluded benefits or non-covered services
- Insurance denial or decision not to pay from submitted documentation
- Limited or Catastrophic health insurance plan coverage

You may find yourself in a situation where your insurance company is denying payment on your claim or not giving approval for services that a physician has ordered for you. As a consumer, you have the right to appeal any insurance denial and provide additional information that may allow the insurance carrier to reverse their original determination.

In order to do this, you will need to determine the specific reason for the denial. You will need to submit your appeal based on that specific reason within the timelines defined for your appeal to be considered. For example, if the denial is based on not being a "covered benefit" under your insurance plan, trying to convince the insurance plan that the requested procedure or treatment is "medically necessary" will not affect the final outcome of the appeal as it does not address the denial reason. PAF has a publication entitled *Your Guide to the Appeals Process* that may be beneficial if you are finding it necessary to submit an appeal.

If your plan details do not cover your medical needs or you have a limited benefits plan (also known as a "Catastrophic" health plan), consider these options for accessing the care you need:

- Negotiate with your provider for a self-pay or prompt-pay discount if you must pay yourself without insurance help.

- Utilize resources that provide a "cost calculator" for common procedures when negotiating a discounted rate. (Examples: consumerreports.org/health/insurance/health-insurance.htm or lifehappens.org).

- Use free clinics for routine and primary care.

- Utilize state and federal programs for free Pap smears, mammograms, breast and cervical cancer screenings, and diagnostic services.

- Conversion Plan: Upon termination of the 18-month period of COBRA coverage, the plan member may be able to convert the policy to a private limited benefit policy. Contact your insurer.

- Group Health Benefits/COBRA: Determine if health coverage is available through you or your spouse's/partner's employment, or through a COBRA plan if you or your spouse/partner has recently left employment. For additional information you can visit dol.gov or call 1-866-444-3272.

- Consider upgrading your plan or choosing another plan with benefits that better match your needs during the next Open Enrollment period.

Section 4: Protections

YOU CANNOT BE DENIED INSURANCE DUE TO YOUR HEALTH

The need to maintain or secure health coverage is a concern to everyone, but when you are diagnosed with a progressive or chronic disease, it is critical. Having insurance coverage ensures that you are able to continue necessary medical treatment both now and in the future. Thanks to the Affordable Care Act, you cannot be denied enrollment in a health plan due to your current or past medical history.

PRIVACY

You have privacy rights under federal law, passed in 1996, that protects your health information. These rights are important for you to know. As a consumer, you can exercise these rights, ask questions about them, and file a complaint if you think your rights are being denied or your health information is not being protected.

Who must follow this law?

- Most doctors, nurses, pharmacies, hospitals, clinics, nursing homes, and many other healthcare providers
- Health insurance companies, HMOs, and most employer group health plans

- Certain government programs that pay for healthcare, such as Medicare and Medicaid

To learn more about the protections under HIPAA, visit <u>dol. gov</u> or call 1-866-444-3272.

CONSOLIDATED OMNIBUS BUDGET RECONCILIATION ACT (COBRA)

COBRA is a federal law that requires certain employers with 20 or more full-time employees or equivalent in the previous 12 months to offer continuation of healthcare coverage to qualified beneficiaries. Under COBRA, the status of the qualifying beneficiary and the qualifying event determines the length of time COBRA coverage is available. The usual length of COBRA coverage is 18 months unless there are other circumstances or state laws that would require the employer to extend the benefits to a maximum of 36 months.

Some of these circumstances include:

- A Social Security Disability award is a requirement for patients seeking 11-month COBRA extension. To qualify, you would need to be deemed disabled by Social Security Administration (SSA) within 60 days of enrolling in COBRA, and you must notify your previous employer.

- Divorce, death, legal separation, or when a dependent child grows older and is no longer considered a dependent may qualify you for the full 36 months. If the employee becomes entitled to Medicare coverage prior to leaving employment, their family members can qualify for up to 36 months of COBRA coverage.

- If an employee becomes entitled to Medicare prior to leaving employment, his or her family member may qualify for up to 36 months of coverage. If an individual is eligible for coverage under a COBRA plan, the state may provide benefits in the form of premium payments and allow the individual to maintain current coverage rather than be covered by Medicaid benefits.

To find out if your state offers this benefit, you can contact your local Medicaid office. Some states have rules in place that require employers with less than 20 employees to offer "mini-COBRA." The amount of coverage varies by state, and you must contact the insurer directly to enroll. For more information, contact your human resource department or visit cobrahealth.com.

COST OF COBRA

You will find that the premium for COBRA is more expensive than you were paying while employed, as the employer no longer pays their portion of the premium payment. Under COBRA you have to pay up to 102% of the premium, including an administration fee. Some states offer premium assistance through their Medicaid program; this may be an option if you qualify for Medicaid and are struggling to afford your COBRA premiums. You can find out whether your state has a provision that allows this by contacting your local Medicaid office. There may be other programs offered through your state or federal government; inquire with your Department of Labor or local state Department of Insurance. It is your responsibility to pay your premiums.

Read all paperwork you receive carefully. This will tell you where to send your insurance premium payments and whether or not you will receive monthly bills. Failure to pay the premium on time will cancel the coverage with no option for reinstatement. For additional information on COBRA, you can visit dol.gov/ebsa or call 1-866-444-3272.

Section 5: Definitions

Benefit limits, also known as Capped Benefits, can come in many ways, such as annual, lifetime, or limit on a specific treatment.

The Affordable Care Act (also known as ObamaCare) stops insurers from setting yearly or lifetime dollar limits on essential benefits. Since 2014, health insurance companies have had to follow new rules on what benefits can be subject to dollar limits and what dollar limits can be set. Let's take a look at the new rules on annual and lifetime limits and how they apply to something the new law calls "essential health benefits."

The Affordable Care Act's Ten Essential Health Benefits include:

1. **Ambulatory patient services (outpatient care)**: care you receive without being admitted to a hospital, such as at a doctor's office, clinic, or same-day ("outpatient") surgery center. Also included in this category are home health services and hospice care. (Note: some plans may limit coverage to no more than 45 days.)

2. **Emergency services (trips to the emergency room)**: care you receive for conditions that could

lead to serious disability or death if not immediately treated, such as accidents or sudden illness. Typically, this is a trip to the emergency room and includes transport by ambulance. You cannot be penalized for going out-of-network or for not having prior authorization.

3. **Hospitalization (treatment in the hospital for inpatient care)**: care you receive as a hospital patient, including care from doctors, nurses, and other hospital staff, laboratory and other tests, medications you receive during your hospital stay, and room and board. Hospitalization coverage also includes surgeries, transplants, and care received in a skilled nursing facility, such as a nursing home that specializes in the care of the elderly. (Note: some plans may limit skilled nursing facility coverage to no more than 45 days.)

4. **Maternity and newborn care**: care that women receive during pregnancy (prenatal care), throughout labor, delivery, and post-delivery, and care for newborn babies.

5. **Mental health services and addiction treatment**: inpatient and outpatient care provided to evaluate, diagnose, and treat a mental health condition or substance abuse disorder. This includes behavioral health treatment, counseling, and psychotherapy. (Note: some plans may limit coverage to 20 days each year. Limits must comply with state or federal parity laws. Read this document for more information on mental health benefits and the Affordable Care Act.)

6. **Prescription drugs**: medications that are prescribed by a doctor to treat an illness or condition. Examples include prescription antibiotics to treat an infection or medication used to treat an ongoing condition, such as high cholesterol. At least one prescription drug must be covered for each category

and classification of federally approved drugs; however, limitations do apply. Some prescription drugs can be excluded. "Over the counter" drugs are usually not covered even if a doctor writes you a prescription for them. Insurers may limit drugs they will cover, covering only generic versions of drugs where generics are available. Some medicines are excluded where a cheaper, equally effective medicine is available, or the insurer may impose "step" requirements. (Expensive drugs can only be prescribed if doctor has tried a cheaper alternative and found that it was not effective.) Some expensive drugs will need special approval.

7. **Rehabilitative services and devices**: rehabilitative services (help recovering skills, like speech therapy after a stroke) and habilitative services (help developing skills, like speech therapy for children) and devices to help you gain or recover mental and physical skills lost to injury, disability, or a chronic condition. (This also includes devices needed for "habilitative reasons.") Plans have to provide 30 visits each year for either physical or occupational therapy or visits to the chiropractor. Plans must also cover 30 visits for speech therapy, as well as 30 visits for cardiac or pulmonary rehab.

8. **Laboratory services**: testing provided to help a doctor diagnose an injury, illness, or condition, or to monitor the effectiveness of a particular treatment. Some preventive screenings, such as breast cancer screenings and prostate exams, are provided free of charge.

9. **Preventive services, wellness services, and chronic disease treatment**: this includes counseling, preventive care (such as physicals, immunizations, and cancer screenings) designed to prevent or detect certain medical conditions, and care for chronic conditions like asthma and diabetes. (Note: please see our full list of preventive services

for details on which services are covered.) Visit healthcare.gov/preventive-care-benefits/ to learn more.

10. **Pediatric services**: care provided to infants and children, including well-child visits and recommended vaccines and immunizations. Dental and vision care must be offered to children younger than 19. This includes two routine dental exams, an eye exam, and corrective lenses each year.

While all qualified plans must offer the ten essential benefits, the scope and quantity of services offered under each category can vary. Each qualified plan must offer essential health benefits, which overall are equal to the scope of benefits typically covered by employers, as shown by a Department of Labor survey of employer-sponsored coverage.

Your plan may have a benefit limit on coverage outside of the essential benefits list. A benefit limit states how much the health plan will pay for a specific product or service, or the number of services a consumer may receive. (An example would be the number of visits allowed for specialists.) Consumers are responsible to pay for products or services that are considered benefit exclusions and not covered by their insurance plan.

Glossary of Terms

Benefit Exclusions: healthcare products or services that are not considered eligible for coverage (payment) by health insurance plan.

Catastrophic Plan (may be referred to as a Limited Benefit Plan): an insurance policy that provides minimal or "bare bones" coverage for an unexpected illness or injury with lower monthly premiums and caps on out-of-pocket expenses. The limitation on the benefit may be daily or per incident.

Consolidated Omnibus Budget Reconciliation Act (COBRA): a federal law ensuring that employers with 20 or more employees allow for continuation of group health benefits for a temporary period of time under certain circumstances (such as loss or change of employment, reduction in hours worked, death, divorce, or other life events). A qualified beneficiary is any individual covered by the plan the day before the qualifying event. Each beneficiary can elect COBRA independently.

Co-insurance: an insurance policy provision under which both the insured person and the insurer share the covered charges in a specified ration (e.g., 80% by the insurer and 20% by the enrollee).

Co-payment: a cost-sharing arrangement in which the managed care enrollee pays a specified flat amount for a specific service (such as $15 for an office visit or $10 for each prescription drug). Typically it does not vary with the cost of the service, unlike co-insurance, which is based on a percentage of charges. You may see a variation in non-formulary drug co-pays, which are based on a percentage of the total cost.

Deductibles: amounts required to be paid by the insured under a health insurance contract before benefits become payable.

Discounted fee-for-service: an agreed-upon rate for service between the provider and payer that is usually less than the provider's full fee. This may be a fixed amount per service or a percentage discount. Providers generally accept such contracts because they represent a means of increasing their volume or reducing their chances of losing volume.

Medicaid: a federal and state-funded program that is administered by the individual states. You must meet one of the eligibility criteria (aged, blind, disabled, or under age 19) for the program, as well as the income and asset requirements. There are no national guidelines governing the program, so eligibility requirements vary from state to state. For further information you can contact your local Medicaid office or visit cms.hhs.gov to research the benefits available in your state.

Non-covered service or insurance denials: can be a result of a pre-existing health condition, benefit exclusion of the plan, or not obtaining pre-authorization prior to receiving a service.

Out-of-network: issues that occur when a member uses a hospital, physician, or other providers who do not have a contract with the insurance plan. Depending on the provider, you would be subject to balance billing, the difference between what the provider charges and your insurance pays. If you belong to a HMO health plan, there is no benefit if you use non-participating providers unless an exception is made by the health insurance plan.

Out-of-pocket costs: the amounts for healthcare products or services which members are responsible to pay. Out-of-pocket costs include co-payments, co-insurance and deductibles, as well as the insurance premium.

Pharmacy benefits: how your insurance will cover prescription medications. There are a variety of pharmacy benefits such as:

- Benefit Limits or Caps determine how much the insurance plan will pay for specific healthcare products or services or the quantity of services a consumer may receive.

- Generic-only coverage which does not cover brand name drugs but allows for medicine that is the chemical equivalent of a brand-name drug.

- Off-Formulary drugs are medications being prescribed for you but are not on your insurance formulary.

- Off-Label drugs are medications being prescribed for you that have received FDA approval but not for your specific diagnosis.

- Non-covered benefits are for a requested medication not eligible for payment through the health insurance plan.

- Specialty or high-tier drugs are a list of medications determined by the insurance plan that are assigned different levels of cost share and co-payments.

Pre-authorization (prior authorization): determined by each health insurance plan and may require that their members receive approval before undergoing specific medical treatments, tests, or surgical procedures.

Premium: the amount paid to an insurer for providing coverage, typically paid on a periodic basis (monthly, quarterly, etc.).

Prevailing charge: a fee based on the customary charges for covered medical insurance services. In Medicare payments for services or items, it is the maximum approved charge allowed.

Reasonable charge: a method used by Medicare to determine reimbursement for items or services not yet covered under any fee schedule. Reasonable charges are usually determined by the lowest of the actual charge, the prevailing charge in the locality, the physician's customary charge, or the carrier's usual payment for comparable services.

Reimbursement: the actual payment received by providers or patients for benefits covered under an insurance plan.

Usual, customary, and reasonable (UCR) charges: a calculation by a managed care plan of what it believes is the appropriate fee to pay for a specific healthcare product or service, in the geographic area in which the plan operates. "Usual" refers to the individual physician's fee profile, equivalent to Medicare's "customary" charge screen. "Customary" refers to a percentile of the pattern of charges made by physicians in a given locality. "Reasonable" is the lesser of the usual or customary screens.

Section 6: Patient Resources

PAF seeks to empower patients across the country to take control of their healthcare. You may find yourself in a position as many other Americans who have difficulty affording their high out-of-pocket medical costs. The following section will offer resources to help you locate assistance programs that may be able to help you offset these cost.

A more comprehensive interactive tool is available on the PAF website at patientadvocate.org/underinsured. You can answer a few simple questions and obtain a personalized listing of specific resources matched to your needs.

RESOURCES FOR DENTAL

National Foundation of Dentistry for the Handicapped

1-855-242-1272 | 1800dentist.com/national-foundation-of-dentistry-for-handicapped

American Dental Association provides a listing of accredited dental schools. May be an option for discounted service.

1-312-440-2500 | ada.org

RESOURCES FOR VISION

EyeCare America provides free eye care educational materials and facilitates access to eye care at no out-of-pocket cost.

1-800-222-3937 | eyecareamerica.org

New Eyes for the Needy helps improve the vision of poor children and adults in the United States by providing new or recycled donated glasses.

1-973-376-4903 | neweyesfortheneedy.org

Vision USA provides basic eye health and vision care services free of charge to uninsured, low-income people and their families.

1-800-766-4466 | aoa.org/visionusa.xml

RESOURCES FOR HEARING

Hear Now is a national nonprofit program committed to assisting those permanently residing in the U.S. who are deaf or hard of hearing and have no other resources to acquire hearing aids.

1-800-328-8602 | starkeyhearingfoundation.org

CO-PAY ASSISTANCE PROGRAMS

These programs are set up to assist patients with insurance that have co-pays for chemotherapy or prescription medications. Every program has its own guidelines. You can contact the organization for eligibility criteria. The contact information is provided below.

Patient Advocate Foundation's Co-Pay Relief
1-866-512-3861 | copays.org

Healthwell Foundation
1-800-675-8416 | healthwellfoundation.org

Patient Access Network Foundation
1-866-316-7263 | patientaccessnetwork.org

Good Days
1-877-968-7233 | gooddaysfromcdf.org

Patient Services Incorporated
1-877-968-7233 | patientservicesinc.org

Leukemia and Lymphoma Society
1-877-557-2672 | lls.org/copay

Cancer Care Co-Pay Assistance Foundation
1-866-552-6729 | cancercarecopay.org

Caring Voice Coalition, Inc.
1-888-267-1440 | caringvoice.org

National Organization of Rare Disorders, Inc.
1-800-999-6673 | rarediseases.org

OTHER CO-PAY OPTIONS

NeedyMeds is an informational website that has up-to-date contact and instructions about various pharmaceutical manufacturers' drug assistance programs and a listing of co-pay and state programs.

needymeds.com

FEDERAL PROGRAMS

Veterans' Administration provides a broad spectrum of medical, surgical, and rehabilitation care to its qualified veterans and their dependents. Treatment for services is based on the veteran's financial need.

1-877-222-VETS | va.gov

U.S. Department of Health & Human Services is the United States government's principal agency for protecting the health of all Americans and providing essential human services, especially for those who are least able to help themselves. The Office of the Inspector General U.S. Government Hotline is for individuals to call for complaints regarding Medicare or Medicaid, as well as providing assistance with entitlements, benefits, insurance, and resources.

1-877-696-6775 | cms.hhs.gov

COMMUNITY RESOURCES

Call 2-1-1 for help from the United Way with food, housing, employment, healthcare, counseling and more.

211.org

The American Cancer Society (ACS) offers numerous resources, including printed materials, counseling for patient and their families, and information on lodging for people who may require treatment far from home. Contact your local chapter to find out about resources available in your community. Local ACS offices may offer reimbursement for expenses related to cancer treatment, including transportation, medicine, and medical supplies. Financial assistance is available in some areas.

1-800-227-2345 | cancer.org

Catholic Charities provides assistance for meeting basic needs: mortgage and rent, utilities, food, clothing, medical supplies and prescription drugs, shelter, and transportation. Visit the website to find a local phone number for your area.

1-703-549-1390 | catholiccharitiesusa.org

Salvation Army National Headquarters provides assistance on a case-by-case basis. Contact your local house of worship to inquire for any relief programs.

1-800-378-7272 | salvationarmyusa.org

National Patient Travel Center provides information about all forms of charitable, long-distance medical air transportation and provides referrals to all appropriate sources of help to patients who cannot afford travel for medical care.

1-800-296-1217 | patienttravel.org

National Association of Hospital Hospitality Houses, Inc. provides information on free or low-cost temporary lodging to families or patients who are undergoing treatment away from home.

1-800-542-9730 | nahhh.org

HEALTH INSURANCE RESOURCES

The following resources can provide additional guidance on locating state laws and health insurance options:

- Healthcare.gov is a national website that allows consumers to connect with health insurance plan options available within their state, evaluate, compare and enroll in a plan to meet their needs. Visit online or call 1-800-318-2596 for individual assistance 24 hours a day, 7 days a week.
- For reference guides to health insurance by state, visit einsurance.com/insurance-guide.

ACCESS TO CARE RESOURCES

Clinical trials are a way to access care and provide an option for care for the uninsured or underinsured. Some trials absorb most or all of the treatment cost and can be a cost-effective way to access care.

The National Institute of Health (NIH) offers a broad range of trials.

1-800-411-1222 | nih.gov

The National Cancer Institute (NCI) only offers cancer-related trials.

1-888-624-1937 | nci.gov

EmergingMed offers a free online tool that helps cancer patients find appropriate clinical trials.

1-877-601-8601 | emergingmed.com

The U.S. Department of Health & Human Services, Health Resource and Services Administration (HRSA) can connect you to federally funded health centers regardless of your ability to pay.

1-877-464-4772 | findahealthcenter.hrsa.gov

The Hill-Burton Program requires for certain medical facilities or hospitals to provide free or low-cost care without regard to a patient's ability to pay. Patients should inquire about the possibility of free services before entering the hospital.

1-800-638-0742 | hrsa.gov

If you are concerned by breast or cervical symptoms and need screening services, contact the Breast and Cervical Cancer Program before you seek care.

1-800-232-4636 | cdc.gov/cancer/nbccedp

Disclaimer

Every effort has been made to make this guide as up-to-date as possible; however, change is inevitable. If you find any information that is not current or incorrect in this publication, please notify us, and we will correct it in the next printing. Furthermore, if there are other organizations that are not listed here that you feel would be helpful to others, please contact us at 1-800-532-5274 or email your suggestions to *info@ patientadvocate.org.*

Find the Missing Pieces:

NATIONAL UNINSURED RESOURCE DIRECTORY OF THE PATIENT ADVOCATE FOUNDATION

Acknowledgement

The National Uninsured Resource Directory has been prepared by the Patient Advocate Foundation (PAF), a leading direct patient services organization in the country with a mission to eliminate obstacles for patients trying to access quality healthcare. PAF seeks to safeguard patients through effective mediation, assuring access to care, maintenance of employment, and preservation of their financial stability relative to their diagnosis of life-threatening or debilitating diseases.

Established in 2008, the Patient Action Council is a forum comprised of like-minded pharmaceutical and biotechnology advocacy executives who seek to provide valuable tools to patients and improve healthcare in the United States.

It is the intention of the Patient Action Council and the Patient Advocate Foundation that this publication be an educational tool to inform uninsured consumers of their options and to provide tips on navigating the healthcare system.

Support for this guide came from Patient Action Council Members:

Amgen Oncology
Celgene Corporation
GlaxoSmithKline
Lilly Oncology
Novartis Oncology
Patient Advocate Foundation
Pfizer Inc
Sanofi U.S.

How to use this guide

The National Uninsured Resource Directory is intended to help uninsured individuals and families get connected with valuable resources. Patient Advocate Foundation hopes that patients will ultimately feel more empowered when navigating the complex healthcare system and obtain the access to healthcare or health coverage they need.

This directory outlines basic information, recommendations, and helpful tips for uninsured consumers. Many patients find that having these suggestions handy is helpful when speaking with their providers.

We will divide the issues into four categories: accessing healthcare, the financial cost of treatment, future health insurance coverage options, and how to impact care by non-medical methods.

An advocate is someone who pleads the cause of another, one who defends or maintains a cause or proposal, or one that supports or promotes the interests of another. There are many different types of advocates: a friend or family member, nurses, healthcare professionals, social workers, educators, volunteers, or a team made up of these individuals. An advocate can help you better understand your diagnosis and the financial implications, support you through all aspects of care, educate you on treatment options, locate healthcare providers, and maintain a broad awareness of your situation. Ideally, this allows more energy to be spent on your immediate medical needs and mental well-being during treatment.

We encourage all patients to self-advocate and hope to empower you with the resources to do so in this guide. For those with access to the Internet, a more comprehensive, up-to-date interactive tool is available at patientadvocate.org/uninsured.

Section 1: Who Are the Uninsured?

When a patient is diagnosed with an illness, he or she may quickly learn that they need insurance coverage to access adequate and timely care. For this publication, uninsured is defined as an individual who lacks any form of current health insurance coverage.

Uninsured Americans can represent many diverse populations with a multitude of reasons for their lack of health coverage. It is helpful to recognize that uninsured patients come from all levels of society and may be:

- Young adults (ages 18-34)
- Unemployed or have experienced a change in job status
- Disabled
- Those with early retirement at an age before eligible for Medicare
- Self-employed business owners and household members
- Recently separated military veterans
- Low income earners or those who rely solely on supplemental income disbursements (SSDI, SSI, STD, LTD)

- Workers in small firms/companies
- Full-time workers in companies that do not offer group plans or the plan is cost prohibitive
- College students who have yet to enter the workforce
- People in families with part-time and temporary workers
- Older adults who are not yet able to qualify for Medicare
- Spouse or child(ren) of a person whose employer does not offer a family plan
- People transitioning through various stages in life and may have a gap in insurance

Despite recent healthcare reform efforts, millions of Americans still remain uninsured. Patient Advocate Foundation (PAF) wants you to know that you are not alone when dealing with your healthcare needs. PAF seeks to connect patients with national, state, local, and regional resources that are dedicated to improving access to quality care and decreasing the financial burden of medical treatment.

Section 2: Accessing Healthcare While Uninsured

As an uninsured patient, there may be times that you find yourself having difficulty locating appropriate medical treatment. As you can imagine, health insurance coverage can make a difference in whether and when people get necessary medical care, where they access their care, and how healthy they are able to live overall. People without insurance are more likely to delay or forgo preventive and routine medical care, which may result in poorer health outcomes. In this section, we provide a list of tips for patients to gain and improve their access to care.

THESE SUGGESTIONS MAY HELP YOU ACHIEVE SUCCESS FINDING CARE:

- Utilize state and federal programs for free screenings. Each state offers free annual Pap smears and mammograms through the National Breast and Cervical Cancer Early Detection Program (NBCCEDP). Some states also offer screenings for various other types of cancer as well. If you've been screened prior to a diagnosis, some of these programs offer covered care. To inquire about free screening and diagnostic programs, contact your local Department of Health.

- Apply for Medicaid programs if you meet the eligibility criteria in your state. In the event it is determined that you are eligible for regular Medicaid, you may be able to qualify for other programs available through your state, such as food stamps and energy assistance. You can obtain information on these programs and how to apply by contacting your local Medicaid office.

- Apply for county medical assistance programs if you are denied Medicaid. These programs are not available in every county; however, when available, the program is a coordinated system for the low-income, uninsured residents of the county to access needed medical care on a sliding payment scale or at no cost. Contact your local Department of Health for more information.

- Use free clinics or income-based sliding payment scale clinics for preventative, routine, and primary care.

- Search for a clinical trial that is specific to your diagnosis. Clinical trials provide an avenue to care for the uninsured. Trials frequently absorb most or all of the treatment cost and can be an affordable way to access care. The National Institute of Health (NIH) and National Cancer Institute (NCI) offer a broad range of clinical trials. In order to be pre-screened for these trials, you must call the NCI and NIH to determine if you meet their criteria.

- If you are a suffering from a severe, chronic disease and are seeking major or long-term treatment, check with the closest university or teaching hospital to find out if they have a charity care program. Some larger hospitals will pre-qualify a patient for free or reduced care to decrease the financial burden of treatment.

- For access to physical therapy, rehabilitative and occupational therapy, and treatment for speech, hearing and language-related disorders, you can contact local universities or specialty training centers to see if they offer free/reduced care services. Dental schools, for example, often have clinics where services are offered for free or for a fraction of the cost that a private dentist would charge. As with other access-to-care needs, you can contact clinics and hospitals and inquire about charity care, prompt-pay discounts and payment plans. You may also want to apply for Medicaid should you meet certain eligibility criteria.

IF YOU ARE HAVING DIFFICULTY ACCESSING PRESCRIBED MEDICATIONS OR SUPPLIES, YOU MAY FIND THE FOLLOWING ACTION STEPS HELPFUL:

- Explore discount drug options through large retailers, supermarkets, or pharmacy chains such as Walgreens, Wal-Mart, CVS, or Target. Contact your closest retailer to see if a comparable program exists.

- Consider generic-equivalent medications with your doctor's approval.

- Explore mail-order options.

- Check with your provider to see if he or she can offer you samples of the medication.

- Apply for national or disease-specific drug assistance programs. There are also free or low-cost drug programs. A complete listing is available in the resource section of this publication.

- Apply for state drug assistance programs by contacting your local state insurance commissioner's office. You can find a link to state specific programs at needymeds.org.

- Drug replacement programs may be available to assist you by providing medications directly to your physician's office for your use. Discuss these programs with your treating physician. Many drug manufacturers offer medications to patients who are unable to afford them for free or very minimal cost. Visit needymeds.org to find out if your medications are available.

- If you need assistance with the cost of durable medical equipment (DME) and/or specialty products such as diabetes test strips, wheelchairs, lymphedema sleeves, hearing aids, etc., it is a good idea to first make contact with the manufacturer of the product. Some manufacturers will offer discounts to uninsured patients and/or additional resources. Always inquire if there is a financial assistance program available or if payment arrangements can be made. You may also want to check with local charitable organizations in your area such as The Salvation Army and United Way, as they may have donated items available for purchase at a reduced cost.

WHAT IF I CANNOT GET TO MY APPOINTMENTS?

Many times patients have difficulty managing their basic transportation needs when in the midst of a medical incident. Managing frequent appointments to and from facilities for care, procedures, treatments, and follow-up, as well as trips to pharmacies and drug stores when gathering at-home supplies, can further strain a patient and their family.

It is also not uncommon for patients to have to travel long distances to a treating facility, sometimes requiring an overnight stay and an additional cost of lodging. There are a number of organizations that provide free or reduced-cost transportation, specifically for long-distance travel. Organizations like the National Patient Travel Center, Road to Recovery offered by the American Cancer Society, or Angel Flight can assist in coordinating travel options.

You might also contact a local volunteer network for assistance with local travel. For those who fall under special circumstances, there are specific resources geared to help.

Undocumented citizens and migrant and farm workers face even greater challenges in accessing healthcare, since this population does not qualify for government programs and resources are scarce. Migrant Clinicians and the National Center for Farmworker Health network is a resource available to help find care locations for members of these groups. The federal Office of Minority Health & Health Disparities manages a farm worker health cooperative, which can help locate resources.

It is worth checking whether your local health center and free clinic will serve undocumented patients. Areas with high specialty populations will frequently have local programs geared towards helping these patients. Charity care does exist for this population, however, only in limited sectors of the country, and in most times at the discretion of the provider. Make sure to speak with the doctor's billing office or the patient accounts department of the hospital to inquire about charity care and payment plans.

International citizens who are legal permanent residents of the U.S., qualified aliens, short-time visa holders, or those with satisfactory immigration status who are having difficulty accessing healthcare should contact clinics and facilities to inquire about charity care, prompt-pay discounts, and payment plans. You can also apply for Emergency Medicaid through your local Social Services office or contact your local embassy.

ENHANCING COMMUNICATION WITH YOUR DOCTOR

Open and honest discussions with your medical team can be vital to your ability to access needed care. Historically, patients have not felt like they had the option of open dialogue about the course of treatment, options for alternatives, cost of treatment, and how these may affect the patient and doctor decisions. Medical care providers are now more willing and able to discuss these topics with you and now fully embrace the patient as a critical part in the decision team.

Patients who have a good relationship with their doctor receive better care and are usually happier with the health assistance they receive.

HERE ARE SOME TIPS FOR YOU WHEN YOU TALK TO YOUR DOCTOR:

- Do not be embarrassed to discuss personal issues with your doctors. You are a valuable piece of the decision-making process and have insight and instincts that even your doctor does not. Your doctor wants the best outcome for you as much as you do, so do not be afraid to ask questions, voice concerns, or share information with your provider. Empower yourself to ensure you receive the best possible care.

- Be prepared.

- Have a list specifically identifying current prescriptions, including dosage, vitamins or herbal products you take, even infrequently, and any allergies or previous reactions you have experienced. These will be very valuable to the medical team and allow the doctor to have all the information at the same time. If there are medications that have been prescribed to you but you have not filled, bring that list as well.

- Bring copies of medical records and test results if you have them.

- Write down a list of specific questions you have before your visit. List the most important first to make sure they get answered. Keeping the list handy and in view will keep you from forgetting about the list when the doctor arrives to speak to you.

- Bring a pen with a notepad or paper to be able to write down doctor recommendations or valuable information for your reference later. Medical terminology can be very complex and difficult to recall after your appointment; writing it down in front of the doctor will ensure that you have the information and that the spelling is correct.

- Bring an advocate or caregiver to your appointment. Not only will this person be able to support you through the process; they can help you recall answers to the questions you asked.

- Ask the doctor to provide pictures or drawings that may help you understand recommendations.

- Include financial concerns in your discussion. Nothing is more alarming than trying to recover from surgery or major treatment and being surprised by unexpected expenses. You will want to be honest about your ability to pay and the cost of your care prior to beginning treatment. Discuss what the estimated out-of-pocket costs are for your treatment, any discounts offered by the facility for prompt payment, cash payments, or payment plans, or any local, state, federal, or disease-specific resources that might be available. You should also discuss options for effective and lower cost treatment for items like surgery, imaging services, radiology, and lab work.

- Do not be afraid to seek a second opinion. Your doctor should not be offended by your request, and many will encourage you to seek additional counsel. Frequently, a different point of view can open up a different option for you. Seeking a second opinion is not interpreted as a negative experience with your first doctor.

- Keep detailed logs of all appointments, conversations, treatment recommendations, billing statements, and receipts for your records. If and when you need to reference an item, this log will be invaluable to you.

- Interact with your doctor during the visit, and do not be hesitant to share a little about yourself during the visit. Even if it feels forced at times, being mindful to add some normal social interaction, discussing hobbies, interests, activities, etc. can help the doctor by having some information about your life. It will also help your doctor relate to you as a "real person."

- Thank your doctors, nurses, and office staff when they have been collaborative and helpful. They work in a tough environment, and many are trying to ensure you have the best care while frequently feeling overloaded themselves. Appreciation can go a long way and will help make your visits to the doctor more pleasant.

- Do not be afraid to say NO. Sometimes less is more. As you are the best authority on YOU, you will know when NO is the right answer. In the same vein, do not be afraid to say YES and advocate for a certain path. The best treatment plan is one that is crafted with input from both you and your doctor.

- If you feel there are cultural misunderstandings present that may be impacting care, ask whether the hospital or doctor's office has an onsite patient navigator or advocate who can help you communicate better in an effort to have a better dialogue.

NOTE

Please note that Patient Advocate Foundation provides this information as a courtesy to help you navigate and secure better access to care. We do not endorse any specific resource listed nor have any input on a particular resource's eligibility process or scope of mission.

Section 3: Financial Obstacles

Financial instability leads to stress, which can adversely affect your health as well as your mental well-being. Without the knowledge of what resources may be available, the thought of the long road ahead can often times be unbearable.

Patients can easily deplete an entire life's savings in a short amount of time when faced with a life-threatening illness. What will you do? How are you going to afford your treatment? This section will help you prepare for the financial demands that you may face.

When applying for financial assistance, please recognize that many organizations have specific criteria, which must be met in order to qualify, and some organizations may have other assistance in an area that you do not immediately need.

A creative approach is frequently necessary when utilizing various assistance programs. For example, you may need financial assistance to pay your transportation need, and an organization only provides assistance for your utility bill. It may be beneficial to take advantage of the financial assistance for the utility bill and reallocate your money to pay your transportation need, if the program permits reallocation. Either way, assistance will offset costs in your overall budget to help with that specific financial need.

WHAT DO I DO IF I HAVE UNPAID BILLS?

When you are faced with mounting medical bills, there are several ways you can attempt to negotiate with your healthcare provider for an agreeable resolution. These suggestions may help you achieve success when dealing with financial obligations:

- Request applications for partial or full charity care, waived fees, or donated care by the provider. Some organizations also use the terms financial assistance or financial aid to reference the same reduction in cost. (Note: When applying for these charity programs, most facilities will require that patients first apply and be denied for all public assistance such as Medicaid. You should be prepared for a complex application process and will have to disclose all financial information, to include income and assets for the entire household. The benefit is based on family size and income according to a percentage of the federal poverty limit [FPL]. If your income is too high to be granted a charity discount, then oftentimes the facility will offer a self-pay discount. This is usually a percentage of the total bill, and often the balance can be paid over time with agreeable monthly payment arrangements.)

- Inquire at treating hospitals, facilities, and providers about available discount assistance programs such as prompt-pay discounts, self-pay discounts, cash-pay discounts, or reasonable payment arrangements.

- Utilize resources that provide a "cost calculator" for common procedures when negotiating a discounted rate.

- Some facilities offer Care Credit as an option. This is a special category of personal (unsecured) credit where a patient has a specific period of time, up to 18 months, to pay the bill without any finance charges. Many hospitals will not extend payment plans past 12 months. Care Credit offers an option that may make payments affordable.

- If you are successfully awarded financial assistance through the hospital, check with your other providers, as they may be willing to match the discount provided by the hospital. Be aware, however, that they are not obligated to do so. You will need to contact the billing office of each facility to explain your circumstances and present any documentation of assistance you have already been given. It is important to contact the providers and establish some kind of arrangement with them to avoid collections.

WHAT IF I CANNOT AFFORD THE COST OF LIVING?

If you need help with your housing, apply for Section 8 housing (a voucher/certificate that helps you pay your rent) or public housing or consider moving to a residence with less rent. There are also some private and charity organizations that provide direct financial assistance for rental needs that are listed in the directory.

If you struggle to meet your monthly utility payments, contact the Department of Social Services to see if your state has a Low Income Heating Energy Assistance Program (LIHEAP). The Department of Social Services may also be able to refer you to available charity programs or organizations that offer utility relief. For example, HeatShare is administered by the Salvation Army and provides emergency energy assistance on a year-round basis. Funds are used for natural gas, oil, propane, wood, electricity, and emergency furnace repairs. You can also ask your doctor to write a letter of medical necessity to the utility company, as they may be more willing to work with you on a compassionate level due to your diagnosis. Lastly, you may contact the State Utilities Commissioner's office to request their review of a compassionate appeal.

If you could use help with the cost of food, there are places to turn to in your region. Contact your local Department of Social Services to apply for food stamps. Those who are eligible for the food stamp program will receive a plastic card that is swiped just like a debit or credit card.

You may also contact your local churches for food pantries or the United Way to locate food banks in your area. You do not have to be a member of a specific church to benefit from their food programs.

If you are in need of help with your mortgage, call your bank or mortgage lender early and try to work out payment arrangements. Consider selling, refinancing, taking out a second mortgage, taking a reverse mortgage, or establishing an equity line of credit. Be honest about your circumstances when talking to them about your options. Mortgage lenders are more cooperative when approached early.

In general, most assistance organizations will not provide financial assistance for secured debt, delinquent taxes, or liens. Secured debt may be an automobile or collateral-backed debt. Your best option for this type of debt would be to work directly with the creditor and ask for alternative payment arrangements for the loan, such as refinancing, deferring payments, or paying only the interest due. Alternate options may be to turn the property back in, sell the property for a profit, or refinance.

ARE YOU UNABLE TO MAKE YOUR UNSECURED DEBT AND CREDIT CARD PAYMENTS?

Contact the creditor to make payment arrangements that involve the most minimal payment you can afford. Be specific in the amount that you are able to afford. If you are unable to establish reasonable payment arrangements directly with the lender, contact a consumer credit counseling service for assistance. Charitable organizations do not typically assist you with making these payments.

Consider debt consolidation as an option. Credit counselors can assist you to consolidate and are able to negotiate lower interest rates and payment arrangements. It is recommended that you only contact those companies that are nonprofit.

If you are managing student loan payments through a federally-backed program, contact your student loan servicer, as there are numerous programs that can give temporary relief, including deferments, forbearance, graduated payment plans, income-contingent payment plans, and interest-only payments.

MyMoney.gov is a helpful source for all ages that provides everyday living financial guidance, education, calculators, and resources. The site helps citizens take control of their finances and gives tips for dealing with credit, over-extended expenses, and how to manage your debt.

Do not forget your medical bills while filing your taxes. Many medical expenses are tax deductible, including mileage for trips to and from medical appointments, out-of-pocket costs for treatment, prescription drugs, medically prescribed equipment, and the cost of meals during medical visits. Keep all documents and records of payment and receipts for your tax professional to apply to your specific scenario.

For all financial related matters, patients may contact Patient Advocate Foundation for assistance locating specific financial resources in your state and county. Patient Advocate Foundation's case managers serve as an advocate on your behalf and can further locate resources that may be available to help.

NOTE

Please note that Patient Advocate Foundation provides this information as a courtesy to help you navigate potential aid. We do not endorse any specific financial resource nor have any input on a resource's eligibility process.

Section 4: Gaining Health Insurance

Whether you have been uninsured for a long time or have recently become uninsured, there are multiple options for you to gain access to health insurance. This chapter will discuss your options for coverage, various forms and types of health insurance plans, and how to understand the specific plan you receive, all to help you choose the best option for coverage to meet your healthcare needs.

Despite your current or past health condition, it is in your best interest to obtain health insurance coverage if at all possible. Insurance coverage provides easier access to care, and you will have more doctors to choose from, since many doctors do not treat uninsured patients.

In addition, insurance gives you and your family protection against a future unexpected health crisis, which could potentially leave you struggling with an exorbitant amount of medical debt. All health insurance plans must cover preventive services and common screenings that may help you find medical concerns as early as possible, giving you more options for treatment and care. Gaining coverage with a health plan that includes dependents and household members ensures they are protected as well.

The sooner you and your family are set up on an insurance plan, the better. Patient Advocate Foundation has found that financial resources, including charity care programs, are becoming fewer in number and more limited in the financial assistance they can provide. Resources are struggling to meet the increased demand due in part to the state of the economy, raised numbers of patients in need, increases in treatment costs, changes in regulation and legislation, and increased complexity in the health system. There is no guarantee as an uninsured patient that an assistance program will be available to you or that you will meet the eligibility criteria, and having insurance is a way to protect yourself and your health.

DO I QUALIFY FOR HEALTH INSURANCE? HOW DO I FIND A PLAN?

Visit Healthcare.gov

Obtain complete information on using the Affordable Care Act Marketplace and the state insurance exchanges.

healthcare.gov/quick-guide

HAVE YOU BEEN DEEMED DISABLED BY THE SOCIAL SECURITY ADMINISTRATION?

If you answered yes:

- You may qualify for Medicaid through your state.
- If you do not qualify for Medicaid, you will become Medicare eligible once you have received Social Security benefits for 29 months or turned 65.
- If you recently stopped working due to your disability and elected COBRA benefits, you may be eligible for an 11-month extension of COBRA in order to bridge the gap between the normal 18-month COBRA period and the waiting period for Medicare.

Are you married?

If yes: if you are married at the time you become disabled and your spouse has an employer group health policy, you may be eligible to elect coverage under your spouse's policy and may not be subjected to a pre-existing condition clause if done within a timely fashion.

If you answered no, please review the following questions and answers.

Does your employer offer group benefits?

If yes, you may choose to elect group health insurance benefits upon being hired or during Open Enrollment periods.

Are you under 26 years old?

New healthcare regulations allow parents to cover children under their policy until the age of 26 years old, regardless of student status, employment, or medical history.

Do you have a pre-existing condition?

If no, you may want to shop around for an individual policy through a licensed insurance provider in your area.

If yes, you may qualify for a Pre-Existing Condition Insurance Plan (PCIP). You can reach the Pre-Existing Condition Insurance Plan at 1-866-717-5826 to see if you qualify.

Did you recently lose a job that provided health insurance benefits to you?

If you answered yes, you may be eligible for COBRA benefits.

Did you exhaust your COBRA benefits?

If you answered yes, you may be able to receive a HIPAA eligible plan.

If you have had 18 months of continuous coverage and have exhausted your COBRA benefits, not due to fraud or non-payment of premiums, you have 63 days from the date your COBRA benefits term to elect a HIPAA eligible plan.

For more specific questions pertaining to health insurance options in your area, contact your state's Bureau of Insurance.

COMMON TYPES OF INSURANCE

The Marketplace

Visit healthcare.gov to connect with your state's insurance marketplace.

The Affordable Care Act provides state-specific Health Insurance Exchanges (often called Marketplaces). These Health Insurance Marketplaces are online price comparison websites where consumers can purchase health insurance that counts as minimum essential coverage, receive federal subsidies, and be granted exemptions.

To be eligible for health coverage through the Marketplace, you:

- Must live in the United States
- Must be a U.S. citizen or national (or be lawfully present). Learn about eligible immigration statuses: healthcare.gov/immigrants/immigration-status.
- Can't be incarcerated: healthcare.gov/incarcerated-people

If you have Medicare coverage, you're not eligible to use the Marketplace to buy a health or dental plan. Learn more about Medicare and the Marketplace: healthcare.gov/medicare/medicare-and-the-marketplace.

Marketplaces are available in every state in the U.S. Also known as public exchanges, these government-run online "shopping" hubs are available for individual consumers and small businesses with fewer than 50 full-time employees to compare plan offerings and buy health insurance.

The Marketplaces are governed by individual states, the federal government, or a partnership between the two. Health plan options and legal standards vary by state.

Employer-based insurance

This is insurance offered as a benefit provided by your employer. Insurance premiums may be paid completely or partially by the employer. If the company is small, you may have to pay premiums yourself, but still have access to group policies and group negotiated rates. Employers may offer a variety of plan options, i.e., HMO plans, PPO plans or High Deductible plans.

Individual health plans

Insurance companies sell individual health plans to consumers looking to purchase coverage for their healthcare needs. They do so through the Marketplace or through brokers.

The individual is responsible for the full amount of their premium, and oftentimes these plans are very costly. A person interested in purchasing an individual plan can get full information on their state exchange.

COBRA-Consolidated OMNIBUS Budget Reconciliation Act

If you previously had coverage through your employer, the COBRA law requires continuation coverage to be offered to employees, their spouses, their former spouses, and their dependent children when group health coverage would otherwise be lost due to certain specific events including divorce, loss of "dependent child" status, termination of employment, resignation of employment, or leaving due to illness.

COBRA generally applies to all group health plans maintained by private-sector employers (with at least 20 employees) or by state and local governments. Your employer must provide the information/paperwork within 30 days, and you have 60 days to elect this option. You can be charged up to 102% of the insurance premium (full cost of coverage plus 2% administrative fee).

Medicaid

Medicaid is a federally funded, state-run program that provides medical coverage for individuals and families with limited income and resources that meet certain eligibility criteria. Since Medicaid coverage varies from state to state, a person who is eligible for Medicaid in one state may not be eligible in another state, and the services provided by one state may differ. For more information regarding Medicaid eligibility criteria by state, please visit the Centers for Medicare and Medicaid Services (CMS) website. You can also check with your local Department of Human Services to see if you qualify.

medicaid.gov / cms.gov/medicaidgeninfo/01_overview.asp

Supplemental insurance

You may come across policies that specialize in specific medical areas or medical events. These may also be termed "defined benefit insurance." Dental insurance, vision insurance, and fixed reimbursement policies offered by companies like Aflac are examples of this type of insurance. These policies tend to be simpler to understand because they very specifically define what is included and provide non-negotiable maximums for benefits. Sometimes these policies will reimburse you directly for the covered services rather than paying the provider and many times are processed much quicker than traditional plans. Supplemental policies can help you manage out-of-pocket costs and deductible costs associated with traditional policies. Life Insurance, Short Term Disability, Long Term Disability, Accident, and Hospitalization are some options for this type of insurance.

Spouse policy

Although this is not a separate type of insurance, it is listed here to make patients aware that they may be eligible for insurance benefits as an add-on to their spouse's policy. To find out the options and cost of adding a spouse to a current policy, contact the benefits office of the plan holder. In addition, adult children under the age of 26 may still be eligible under their parent's medical coverage plan.

UNDERSTANDING YOUR PLAN

It is important to take a crucial look at your plan, specifically if you have an option among various plans. For whatever plan you choose, once your coverage begins, it is important to truly understand the specifics of your policy. Many patients end up with excess stress and frustration that could have been prevented with a little upfront education. Plans are extremely complex and are not usually written for easy reading; however, here are some basics to consider:

- Ask questions to ensure you understand your deductible amounts and the co-pays you are financially obligated to pay for prescription tiers, regular office visits, specialists and emergency room visits.

- Be sure to research the doctor you go to, ensuring they are a covered provider by the plan, and whether or not the insurance company considers them a specialist.

- Pay attention to the referral process among doctors in the network and the paperwork that may accompany you seeing a specialist. Many times if these processes are not followed in advance of a visit, you can be responsible for the entire medical visit costs.

- Knowing what your yearly out-of-pocket maximums are can be important in family budgeting. These will vary based on if you are covered as an individual or as a family.

- Knowing what types of services, procedures, or treatment is covered and what is not may affect you and your doctor's decision on treatment.

- When traveling, be sure to pinpoint your coverage options for out-of-state and emergency services when in transit and away from your normal service area.

- Identify how to access your plan's customer service or account information line for when you need to discuss plan and payment issues.

Section 5: Impacting Your Healthcare with Non-Medical Means

There are many lifestyle and diet elements that research has shown can dramatically affect your overall health. Before, during, or after battling a major illness, maximizing your healthy behaviors can impact your need for, access to, and cost of care.

Medical research and the medical community suggest that individuals maintain an overall healthy lifestyle. Listed here are some of the good health guidelines that are tied to lower illness rates and better overall health:

- **Eat a well-rounded and balanced diet**. You should be increasing your vegetable and leafy greens intake, limiting highly processed foods, eating foods that are high in fiber, low in sugar, and low in fat and ensuring you drink plenty of fluids every day.

- **Limit salt intake**. Learn how to read product labels and how to identify salt and sodium amounts in your food. Be aware that many processed foods have extremely high levels of salt, even if they do not taste salty.

- **Ensure you are getting proper vitamins, minerals, and nutrition**. The Vitamins &

Nutrition Center provides accurate information on vitamins and nutrition, research on vitamins, and the different effects of specific vitamin deficiency. Maintaining recommended levels will ensure your body is prepared to keep you healthy.

- **Stop smoking and tobacco use.**

- **Manage your stress level.** Many find that incorporating frequent laughter, relaxation, quiet time, positive influences, and time to explore hobbies can dramatically affect stress levels and your body's response to stress.

- **Limit excessive alcohol intake.**

- **Maintain a healthy weight.** Obesity studies show an increased connection of extra body fat to many major illnesses and diseases. Likewise, individuals who are too far below the recommended weight may have decreased body resources to fight or resist germs, bacteria, and viruses, leading to medical complications.

- **Incorporate exercise and movement into your lifestyle as much as possible.**

- **Protect yourself against germs.** One of the biggest ways to avoid extra germs is to wash your hands thoroughly and often. Cleaning hard surfaces on a regular basis will minimize the spread of germs. Giving yourself access to fresh air will also help to reduce your exposure to harmful bacteria and viruses.

- **Seek preventive and early detection care.** Regular and adequate preventive care has significantly impacted the longevity of individuals and will help keep you healthier in the long run. Routine exams, vaccinations, and screenings are key. Early detection of serious conditions can lower healthcare costs and improve outcomes.

- **Get enough sleep**. Your body functions better when well rested and is better prepared to tackle the challenges of your life when adequate sleep is maintained.

For more detail on these and more tips and guidelines for building a healthy lifestyle, visit cdc.gov/HealthyLiving.

Section 6: Definitions & Insurance-Related Terms

Advocate: "A person or group that acts on your behalf." Frequently advocates will plead the case for another to promote their best interest. There are many different types of advocates, including the patient themselves, and may include friends, family, nurses, healthcare professionals, social workers, educators, volunteers, or any combination of such.

Care Credit: A special category of personal (unsecured) credit where a patient has a specific period of time, up to 18 months, to pay the bill without any financial charges.

Clinical Trial: Medically supervised treatment and care that specifically studies new drugs, combinations of drugs (some already FDA approved for other purposes), and/or treatments to see how well they work – especially when compared with current standard of care treatment. In clinical trials, most or all of the medical costs related to the trial are covered at no cost to the patient, including doctor visits, procedures, and follow-up.

Consolidated Omnibus Budget Reconciliation Act (COBRA): This federal law ensures that employers with 20 or more employees allow for continuation of group health benefits for a temporary period of time under certain circumstances (such as loss or change of employment, reduction in hours worked, death, divorce, or other life events). A qualified beneficiary is any individual covered by the plan the day before the qualifying event. Each beneficiary can elect COBRA independently.

Federal Poverty Limit (FPL) or Poverty Guidelines: The federally designated income threshold measure that functions as a guideline and impacts services for low-income individuals and families. It is calculated each year by the Census Bureau. This dollar number refers to the total gross income for a household, including all methods of income for all earners within the household. The amount allowed within the guidelines varies by the number of persons in a household.

Health Maintenance Organizations (HMOs): This is a managed care plan through an insurance provider in which the enrollee must choose a Primary Care Provider (PCP) who is responsible for managing and coordinating their care. It requires the patient to stay within a contracted network of providers for their healthcare needs. In this type of plan, the patient must get a referral from their PCP to see a specialist.

Insured: A patient who has some form of current insurance coverage for medical treatment. Insurance may be private coverage, federal or state funded programs (Medicare, Medicaid), Active Military or Veterans Assistance, COBRA, University Student Program, Individual Plan, etc.

Medicaid vs. Medicare: Many Americans get these two programs confused or believe they are the same program under different names. Medicaid is a state-run program designed primarily to help those with low income and little or no financial resources. The federal government helps pay for Medicaid, but each state has its own rules about who is eligible and what is covered under Medicaid. Some people may qualify for both Medicare and Medicaid. Medicare is our national health insurance program for people with disabilities, people of any age who have permanent kidney failure, amyotrophic lateral sclerosis (ALS/Lou Gehrig's Disease), and people who are 65 or older. It provides basic protection against the cost of healthcare, but does not cover all medical expenses or the cost of most long-term care.

Medicaid: A federal and state-funded program that is administered by individual states. You must meet one of the eligibility criteria (aged, blind, disabled, or under the age of 19) for the program, as well as the income and asset requirements. There are no national guidelines governing the program, so eligibility requirements vary from state to state. For further information you can contact your local Medicaid office or visit Center for Medicaid Services website at cms.hhs.gov to research the benefits available in your state.

Medicare: A federally funded program for patients who are 65 years or older or who have been receiving Social Security benefits for 24 months.

Preferred Provider Organizations (PPOs): This type of managed care plan contracts with a network of "preferred providers" from which the patient can choose. In this type of plan the patient does not need to select a PCP and does not need a referral to see a specialist.

Pre-Existing Condition: You cannot be denied insurance because you are sick or have an illness.

Uninsured: An individual who lacks current health insurance coverage. At times, you may be considered uninsured if a specific treatment or procedure is not covered under your existing plan.

Section 7: Patient Resources

Patient Advocate Foundation seeks to empower patients across the country to take control of their healthcare. Since you are reading this, you may find yourself in a position like many other Americans who are having difficulty affording their healthcare or obtaining insurance. The following section will offer resources to help you locate assistance programs that may be able to help you.

We have attempted to include a current telephone number in addition to an online contact point for each entry listed; however, most organizations have focused on advancing their website efforts as a primary means of communication about their specific services and patient tools.

We remind you that most local libraries serve as sources of free computer usage with the internet. Many parks and recreation centers, community centers, and senior centers have public computers available for you to access additional online information. If you have an internet-capable device, numerous retail outlets offer complimentary internet on their property, including McDonalds, Panera Bread, Barnes & Noble, Starbucks, Chick-fil-A, and many more. Retail stores like FedEx Kinkos Office, Staples, OfficeMax, and other internet cafes will offer computer and internet access to the public for a rental charge by the hour or less.

A more comprehensive interactive tool is available on the Patient Advocate Foundation website at patientadvocate.org/uninsured. By answering a few simple questions, you can obtain a personalized listing of specific resources matched to your needs.

Every effort has been made to make this guide as up-to-date as possible. Please understand that Patient Advocate Foundation provides this information as a courtesy to help you navigate potential aid, but does not endorse any specific resource nor have any input on a resource's eligibility process.

ACCESS TO CARE RESOURCES

Breast & Cervical Cancer Program

If you are concerned by breast or cervical symptoms and need screening services, contact this program before you seek care.

1-800-232-4636 | cdc.gov/cancer/nbccedp

Disability.gov

A federal website for comprehensive information on disability programs and services in communities nationwide. The site links to more than 14,000 resources from federal, state, and local government agencies, academic institutions, and nonprofit organizations. New information is added daily across 10 main subject areas—Benefits, Civil Rights, Community Life, Education, Emergency Preparedness, Employment, Health, Housing, Technology, and Transportation.

disability.gov

EmergingMed

Offers a free online tool that helps cancer patients find appropriate clinical trials.

1-877-601-8601 | emergingmed.com

Find a free clinic

List maintained by the National Association of Free Clinics, this search tool can help you locate clinics in your area offering free medical services.

1-703-647-7427 | freeclinics.us

Find a health center

The U.S. Department of Health and Human Services website will help you locate federally funded health centers that help you even if you do not have insurance and provide services based on your income. Federally Qualified Health Centers (FQHCs) and Rural Health Clinics provide care to many populations, including those with limited English proficiency, children and youth with special healthcare needs, lesbian, gay, bisexual and transgender patients. Includes checkups, pregnancy care, immunizations and checkups for children, dental care, mental health, and substance abuse care.

1-877-464-4772 | findahealthcenter.hrsa.gov

Hill-Burton Program

By U.S. Department of Health and Human Services. Free and reduced care clinics for individuals and families who cannot afford care. Hill-Burton-assisted facilities include hospitals, nursing homes, and other healthcare facilities.

1-800-638-0742 | hrsa.gov/gethealthcare/affordable/hillburton

Local free clinics and sliding scale clinics

You can visit needymeds.org/freeclinics.taf to locate free clinics and sliding scale clinics in your area. Visitors can search by state or zip code.

National Cancer Institute (NCI)
Offers cancer-related trials.

1-888-624-1937 | nci.gov

Redi-Clinic and Minute-Clinic walk-in clinics

Retail walk-in clinics that offer trained nurse care for many common conditions like colds, eye infections, strep throat, bladder infections, sore throat, physicals, vaccinations and immunizations, and are frequently located near or in pharmacies.

rediclinic.com | minuteclinic.com | takecarehealth.com

The National Institute For Health (NIH)

Offers a broad range of clinical trials.

1-800-411-1111 | nih.gov

Veterans benefits

Provides a broad spectrum of medical, surgical, and rehabilitative care for qualified veterans and their dependents. Treatment for services is based on the veteran's financial need.

1-877-222 8387 or 1-800-827-1000 | va.gov
Veterans Crisis Line: 1-800-273-8255

American Cancer Society (ACS)

Offers numerous resources, including printed material, counseling for patients and their families, and information on lodging for people who may require treatment far from home. Contact your local chapter to find available resources in your area. Local ACS offices may offer reimbursement for expenses related to cancer treatment, including transportation, medicine, and medical supplies. Financial assistance is available in some areas.

1-800-227-2345 | cancer.org

Association of Independent Consumer Credit Counseling Agencies (AICCCA)

The largest national association representing nonprofit credit counseling companies. AICCCA provides a list of nonprofit organizations that provide consumer credit counseling, debt management, housing counseling, bankruptcy counseling, and financial education services for individuals and families experiencing financial distress.

1-866-703-8787 | credithelp4u.org/UNITEDWAY

Aubrey Rose Foundation

Helps families with children who are currently living with a life-threatening medical conditions. Financial grants are awarded to cover outstanding medical bills as a result of treatment, are based on financial need, and can be geographically anywhere in U.S.

1-513-265-5801 | aubreyrose.org

Benefits.Gov

Federal website to help you find the government benefits you qualify for, including housing, food, medical, and many more.

1-800-333-4636 | benefits.gov

Catholic Charities

Connect with a local Catholic Charities office for financial assistance in a number of medical, personal, and living arenas. You do not have to be of the Catholic faith to receive benefits. Provides assistance for meeting basic needs—mortgage and rent, utilities, food, clothing, medical supplies, prescription drugs, shelter, and transportation.

1-800-919-9338 | catholiccharititesusa.org

Debt consolidation

Learn about debt consolidation loans and get quotes for various services. Lending Tree can help you learn how to get out of debt by consolidating loans to lower your payments and paying off debt.

1-800-555-8733 | lendingtree.com/debt-consolidation/advice

Health Cost Helper

Helps patients get an idea of what a fair and average price is for a wide variety of healthcare supplies, procedures and treatments. Includes products, surgeries, imaging, vaccinations, and medical supplies.

1-408-844-4900 | health.costhelper.com

Healthcare Blue Book

The Healthcare Blue Book is a free consumer guide to help you determine fair prices in your area for healthcare services. The Blue Book will help you find fair prices for surgery, hospital stays, doctor visits, medical tests, and much more.

1-615-422-5213 | healthcarebluebook.com

HeatShare

Provides emergency energy assistance on a year-round basis. Funds are used for natural gas, oil, propane, wood, electricity, and emergency furnace repairs.

1-800-842-7279

MyMoney.gov

A helpful source for all ages that provides everyday living financial guidance, education, calculators, and resources. The site helps citizens take control of their finances and gives tips for dealing with credit, over-extended expenses, and how to manage debt.

1-888-696-6639 | mymoney.gov

National Association of Hospital Hospitality Houses, Inc.

Provides information on free or low-cost temporary lodging to families or patients who are undergoing treatment away from home.

1-800-542-9730 | nahhh.org

National Patient Travel Center

Provides information about all forms of charitable, long-distance medical air transportation and provides referrals to all appropriate sources of help to patients who cannot afford travel for medical care.

1-800-296-1217 | patienttravel.org

Partnership for Prescription Assistance

The Partnership for Prescription Assistance helps qualifying patients without prescription drug coverage get the medicines they need for free or nearly free.

1-888-477-2669 | pparx.org

RXHope

RXHope is another clearinghouse option for prescription assistance for low-income U.S. residents.

1-877-267-0517 | rxhope.com

Patient Advocate Foundation

Provides free advocate services by helping patients coordinate resources for their specific medical care needs and financial obligations. Serves patients from all U.S. states.

1-800-532-5274 | patientadvocate.org

Pharmacy Checker

An online resource that helps you identify, locate, and compare reputable online pharmacies. This site also allows patients to compare prices for medications among various pharmacy providers.

pharmacychecker.com

RX Aid Prescription Assistance

Patient assistance programs that aid uninsured patients with getting their prescriptions at low or no cost.

1-877-610-9360 | rxaid.wordpress.com

RXAssist

A comprehensive directory of patient assistance programs run by pharmaceutical companies to provide free medications to people that cannot afford to buy their medicine.

rxassist.org

Salvation Army National Headquarters

Provides assistance on a case-by-case basis, including housing, emergency food, and family service programs. Visit the website for online tools or search by your zip code to find Salvation Army locations near you.

salvationarmyusa.org

Self-pay medical discounts

Pre-negotiated low cost self-pay options for CT scans, MRI scans, and Radiologist services in every state. Not dependent on insurance type or coverage.

1-888-380-6337 | wecaremedicalmall.org

State Pharmaceutical Assistance Programs (SPAP)

Many states have state-sponsored subsidies and discounts for seniors, disabled, uninsured, and others. The National Conference of State Legislatures maintains a list of state-specific prescription programs with a list of eligibility requirements.

1-202-624-5400 | ncsl.org/issues-research/health/state-pharmaceutical-assistance-programs-2011.aspx

State Utilities Commissioners Office

Full contact listing for all utilities commissioners' state offices for all 50 states, provided by the National Association of Regulatory Utility commissioners.

1-202- 898-2200 | naruc.org/commissions.cfm

United Way

A nationwide directory of information referral services for health counseling, legal aid, crisis intervention, financial services, and emergency relief.

1-800-411-8929

In many communities, you can just dial 2-1-1 for United Way help with food, housing, employment, healthcare, counseling, and more.

211.org

HEALTH INSURANCE RESOURCES

Bureau of Insurance for States

A complete list with contact information for each state's Bureau of Insurance can be found.

1-816-783-8500 | naic.org/state_web_map.htm

eHealthInsurance

This is one of the largest online health insurance brokers and offers a number of resources, including a Buyer's Guide that will help consumers assess their needs, understand different policy types, and get competitive quotes from multiple insurance companies. This broker deals with individual, family, and small business plans. EHealthInsurance does not charge consumers a fee to use their services.

1-844-298-4329 | ehealthinsurance.com

Children and teen medical coverage options

Government resource that connects kids and teens to medical coverage, including no-cost or low-cost insurance. Offers assistance in any state. Includes the Children's Health Insurance Program (CHIP) for U.S. citizens and eligible immigrants.

1-877-543-7669 | insurekidsnow.gov

InsureUStoday.org

A website geared towards adding clarity to the new healthcare and medical insurance-related changes as a result of the Patient Protection and Affordable Care Act passed in 2010. Includes a calendar showing the changes that will be gradually implemented through 2018.

1-866-207-8023 | insureustoday.org

Mission of Mercy

Provides free healthcare, free dental care, and free prescription medications to the uninsured, undocumented, and those who "fall through the cracks" of our healthcare system. Clinics in Arizona, Maryland, Pennsylvania, and Texas.

1-301-682-5683 | amissionofmercy.org

HEALTH COVERAGE EDUCATION STATE BY STATE

The Foundation for Health Coverage Education helps you answer questions about what insurance options you qualify for, helps you with enrollment in free and low-cost options, and provides assistance 24 hours a day via an uninsured help line. In addition to a number of coverage resources, they maintain a healthcare options matrix organized by state to help you find the resources in your area.

coverageforall.org

Alaska Native

Alaska Native Medical Center provides services, health information, and resources specifically for Alaska natives.

1-907-563-2662 | anmc.org

American Dental Association

Provides a listing of accredited dental schools. May be an option for discounted services.

1-312-440-2500 | ada.org

Angel Flight

Angel Flight West arranges free air transportation in response to healthcare and other compelling human needs. A nonprofit, volunteer-driven organization that seeks to enable treatment that might otherwise be inaccessible because of geographic limitations.

1-888-426-2643 | angelflight.org

CaringBridge

CaringBridge free websites allow you to create personal, private outlets to ease the burden of keeping family and friends informed. Patients, caregivers, and family members can simplify communication and connect your community during a health journey, saving you time and energy.

1-651-452-7940 | caringbridge.com

Eye Care America

Provides free eye care, educational materials, and facilities to access eye care at no out-of-pocket cost.

1-800-222-3937 | eyecareamerica.org

HearNow

A national nonprofit program committed to assisting those permanently residing in the U.S. who are deaf or hard of hearing and have no other resources to acquire hearing aids.

1-800-328-8602 | starkeyhearingfoundation.org

National Council on Aging/National Center for Senior Benefits Outreach and Enrollment

An advocate service for older Americans with limited means who are not receiving federal or state benefits, helping each to locate and receive benefits to assist in care, food, and living expenses.

1-202-479-1200 | ncoa.org/enhance-economic-security/center-for-benefits

National Energy Assistance Referral (NEAR) Project

Provides contacts for assistance paying your utility bills and locating federal Low-Income Home Energy Assistance Program (LIHEAP) providers in your location.

1-866-674-6327 | benefits.gov/benefits/benefit-details/623

National Dental Lifeline Network

This dental-focused organization provides access to comprehensive dental services for people with disabilities or who are elderly or medically at-risk.

1-303-534-5360 | nfdh.org

National Hispanic Prenatal Hotline (in Spanish)

The National Hispanic Prenatal Helpline (NHPH) focuses on addressing barriers to receiving prenatal care services among Hispanics by providing access to culturally and linguistically proficient services and information. The NHPH aims to raise awareness concerning the problems of infant mortality, to promote healthy behaviors, and to motivate all women to enter prenatal care early in their pregnancy.

1-800-504-7081

National Indian Health Board

This group represents and assists tribal governments that provide healthcare delivery systems, clinics, and treatment facilities for persons of Indian heritage.

1-202-507-4070 | nihb.org

National Patient Travel Center

The National Patient Travel HELPLINE provides information about all forms of charitable, long-distance medical air transportation and provides referrals to all appropriate sources of help available in the national charitable medical air transportation network.

1-800-296-1217 | patienttravel.org

New Eyes for the Needy

Helps improve the vision of poor children and adults in the United States by providing new or recycled donated glasses.

1-973-376-4903 | neweyesfortheneedy.org

Office of Minority Health

Focused on health-related issues for African Americans, American Indians, Alaska Natives, Asian Americans, Hispanic and Latino persons, Native Hawaiians, and Pacific Islanders. This office can provide direction to specific resources to aid in health needs.

1-800-444-6472 | minorityhealth.hhs.gov

Older adults benefits

Benefits Check Up is a free service for adults over age 55 to better identify benefits that cover prescription drugs, healthcare, housing, transportation, utilities, and other basic needs.

1-202-479-1200 | benefitscheckup.org

Road to Recovery

Road to Recovery offered by the American Cancer Society is a program that provides transportation to and from treatment for people who have cancer and do not have a ride or are unable to drive themselves. Volunteer drivers donate their time and use their cars to assist patients.

1-800-227-2345

The National Long-Term Care Ombudsman Resource Center

This national help line can assist you when dealing with issues of long-term care.

1-202-332-2275

Vision USA

Provides basic eye health and vision care services free of charge to uninsured, low-income people and their families.

1-800-766-4466 | aoa.org/visionusa.xml

UNDOCUMENTED, MIGRANT, SEASONAL AND IMMIGRANT SPECIFIC RESOURCES

Catholic Charities Immigration and Refugee Services of Florida

Dedicated to the needs of the newest members of our society by providing various services targeting the specific needs for the Florida immigrant community.

1-800- 411- 0714 | cirsorl.org

Escort National Migrant Hotline

The National Migrant Education Hotline is free and accessible to migrant farmworkers and their families anywhere in the United States. The calls are answered by hotline specialists 24 hours a day, seven days a week.

1-800-451-8058 | escort.org

Harvest of Hope Foundation for migrant farm workers

The Harvest of Hope Foundation provides migrant farm workers and their families with emergency relief, education, transportation assistance, housing assistance, clothing, medical, dental, vision, and financial assistance. Assists families throughout the United States.

1-800-234-8848 / 1-888-922-4673 | harvestofhope.net

Health center locator

Patients can contact the national primary clinic network. Visit the sites below for assistance locating a medical provider.

findahealthcenter.hrsa.gov/Search_HCC.aspx
migrantclinician.org

North Carolina Farm Worker Institute

The Farmworker Institute is a project of the N.C. Council of Churches' Farmworker Ministry Committee in collaboration with the N.C. Office of the National Farm Worker Ministry.

1-919-828-6501 | ncfarmworkers.org

Office of Minority Health & Health Disparities (farm worker health)

A combined national effort to provide opportunities for migrant health providers and others who work with the population to enhance skills, create networking and collaboration opportunities, and identify additional resources, program models, and effective training for the more efficient provision of healthcare services to farm workers.

1-404-498-2320 | cdc.gov/omhd/AMH/farmworker.htm

LOCAL COMMUNITY RESOURCES

This guide provides an overview of national resources; however, there is likely to be additional resources in your state, county, city, and neighborhood. When searching in your local phonebook or community directory, state and city government resources may be contained in the following departments: Social Services, Department of Welfare, Health and Human Services, Community Services Board, Community Health, or Health and Family Services.

When looking at local charity programs, consider contacting local chapters of the Red Cross, The Salvation Army, Lutheran Social Services, Jewish Social Services, Catholic Charities, churches or synagogues, fraternal organizations, and civic-minded groups. Depending on the program and specific service, many times you do not need to be a member or affiliated with their specific beliefs to receive services. Many other programs will be listed under Social Service Organizations in the phone book. You may also look into labor unions and social organizations to which any family member belongs.

There are also many disease-specific organizations and charity programs that assist people in their battle against a particular illness or ailment. Speaking to your care provider and medical staff can point you in the direction of well-known programs relevant to your case.

Section 8: Quick Reference

If you are uninsured and unable to access health insurance either through a public program or private insurance provider, there are a few options for you in order to access healthcare:

FREE CLINICS

You may qualify for free primary care services based on your income and assets. Free clinics often have programs to assist with the cost of medications as well. In order to locate a free clinic near you, call or visit the National Association of Free Clinics website.

1-703-647-7427 | nafcclinics.org

SLIDING SCALE FEE CLINICS

These federally funded clinics offer primary care services on a sliding payment scale based on the patient's income and assets.

1-877-464-4772 | findahealthcenter.hrsa.gov

UNIVERSITY OR TEACHING HOSPITALS

If you are suffering from a severe, chronic disease such as cancer and are seeking major or long-term treatment, check with the closest university or teaching hospital to find out if they have a charity care program. Some larger hospitals will pre-qualify a patient for free or reduced care to decrease the financial burden of treatment.

PATIENT ASSISTANCE PROGRAMS

Programs offered through pharmaceutical companies that are designed to help uninsured patients gain access to medications for free.

SCREENING PROGRAMS

Take advantage of preventive screenings—they can make a difference for future care. Ask your local Health Department about free screening programs such as the Breast and Cervical Cancer Early Detection Program. If diagnosed through these programs, patients will be referred to covered future treatment options.

DO I QUALIFY FOR HEALTH INSURANCE? HOW DO I FIND A PLAN?

Have you been deemed disabled by the Social Security Administration?

If you answered yes:

- You may qualify for Medicaid through your state.

- If you do not qualify for Medicaid, you will become Medicare eligible once you have received Social Security benefits for 24 months or turned 65.

- If you recently stopped working due to your disability and elected COBRA benefits, you may be eligible for an

11-month extension of COBRA in order to bridge the gap between the normal 18-month COBRA period and the waiting period for Medicare.

Are you married?

If yes, if you are married at the time you become disabled and your spouse has an employer group health policy, you may be eligible to elect coverage under your spouse's policy and may not be subjected to a pre-existing condition clause if done within a timely fashion.

If you answered no:

- Does your employer offer group benefits?

- If yes, you may choose to elect group health insurance benefits upon being hired or during Open Enrollment periods.

Are you under 26 years old?

New healthcare regulations allow parents to cover children under their policy until the age of 26 years old, regardless of student status, employment, or medical history.

Do you have a pre-existing condition?

If no, you may want to shop around for an individual policy through a licensed insurance provider in your area.

If yes, you may qualify for a Pre-Existing Condition Insurance Plan (PCIP). You can reach the Pre-Existing Condition Insurance Plan at 1-866-717-5826 to see if you qualify.

Did you recently lose a job that provided health insurance benefits to you?

If you answered yes, you may be eligible for COBRA benefits.

Did you exhaust your COBRA benefits?

If you answered yes, you may be able to join a HIPAA eligible plan.

If you have had 18 months of continuous coverage and have exhausted your COBRA benefits, not due to fraud or non-payment of premiums, you have 63 days from the date your COBRA benefits term to elect a HIPAA eligible plan.

For more specific questions pertaining to health insurance options in your area, contact your state's Bureau of Insurance.

Affording the cost of treatment

Whether you're receiving financial assistance for healthcare or not, oftentimes treatment can be very expensive. Here are a few strategies patients can use to manage their medical debt:

- **Look for prompt-pay discounts**. Offer the medical facility a specific amount of money upfront. Some facilities may be willing to accept a smaller amount of money if it means they will collect at the time services are rendered.

- **Apply for financial assistance**. Ask your provider if they have an application you can complete to receive a discount or write-off on your accounts.

- **Arrange an affordable payment plan**. Speak with the facility's billing department to negotiate a monthly payment plan that is feasible for your budget to prevent accounts from going to a collection agency.

- **Participate in screening programs**. Ask your local Health Department about free screening programs such as the Breast and Cervical Cancer Early Detection Program. If diagnosed through these programs, patients will be referred to covered treatment options.

- **Manage your cost during treatment**. By asking questions and talking to your doctors, you can frequently find quality care at an equal or lower price. Walk-in retail clinics (like Minute Clinic and RediClinic), ambulatory surgery centers, outpatient services, and stand-alone imaging and blood diagnostic facilities, for example, can all be less expensive than the same services at hospitals and the doctor's office.

- **Reduce future and current medical costs through a healthy lifestyle**. Many patients see a reduction in their need for medications and medical care by improving their health in general through lifestyle and non-medical means. Be sure to maintain healthy habits when it comes to diet, exercise, weight, social behaviors, and stress management. These can not only save dollars in terms of necessary treatment, but will also give your body the best internal tools when responding to any needed medication or medical action.

Affording your prescriptions

When undergoing treatment for a major illness or maintaining ongoing medication, affording your prescriptions can be difficult when uninsured. A patient's pharmacy needs can quickly put a drain on living expenses and a financial budget.

When speaking to your doctor, be sure to ask about lower cost and comparable medication alternatives, the use of generic brands, bulk discounts, and access to medication samples to ease the burden of cost.

In addition, these assistance programs may be able to aid in the cost of your prescriptions:

- **Pharmacy Checker**: an online resource that helps you identify, locate, and compare reputable online pharmacies. Also allows patients to compare prices for medications among various pharmacy providers.

  1-718- 554-3067 | pharmacychecker.com

- **RXAssist**: a comprehensive directory of patient assistance programs run by pharmaceutical companies to provide free medications to people that cannot afford to buy their medicine.

  rxassist.org

- **State Pharmaceutical Assistance (SPAP)**: Many states have state-sponsored subsidies and discounts for seniors, the disabled, uninsured, and others. The National Conference of State Legislatures maintains a list of state-specific prescription programs with a list of eligibility requirements.

  1-202-624-5400 | ncsl.org/issues-research/health/state- pharmaceutical-assistance-programs-2011.aspx

- **Drug assistance cards/discount pharmacy cards**: These discount cards are offered to patients free of charge and give additional discounts on the out-of-pocket cost of medications. These cards tend to be easy to use and do not require forms to fill out or waiting periods to use. Many are offered by the pharmacy directly, including Kmart, Costco, Walgreens, Rite Aid, etc., or offered as a result of a community partnership. FamilyWize, YourRXCard, and NationalDrugCard are examples of discount cards not tied to any specific pharmacy.

YOUR RIGHTS WHEN IT COMES TO MEDICAL CARE

As an uninsured patient, you have the right to emergency care through emergency rooms in hospitals. However, there are federally defined situations that constitute an "emergency" and specifically do not include preventive, normal illness, and ongoing treatment.

Your right to treatment is not solely based on the fact that you arrive at the emergency room for care, and you may be refused at the emergency room without insurance if your immediate situation does not meet the definitions outlined in federal law. Once your immediate situation has been stabilized, the hospital may elect to transfer or discharge you for further non-emergency care.

Pregnant women in labor, where delivery is imminent, are eligible for care under the emergency definition.

There are many resources online that can further explain, define, and help you to understand your emergency care rights.

U.S. Legal Inc.

U.S. Legal Inc. is an easy to understand, plain language resource designed for consumers, small business, attorneys, corporations, or anyone in need of legal information, products, or services.

1-877-389-0141

National Conference of State Legislators

When insurance coverage is a viable option for you, there are new laws that protect your right to be eligible for coverage, removing the ability for an insurance company to deny you coverage for previous health conditions. To stay abreast of healthcare changes and proposed changes in your state, the National Conference of State Legislators can point you to resources specific to your area.

1-202-624-5400 | ncsl.org

InsureUSToday.org

Healthcare is a constantly evolving system with frequent and sometimes dramatic changes. Patients can visit this website or call to keep up-to-date with the federal changes and a timeline of implementation.

1-866-207-8023 | insureustoday.org

MANAGING YOUR HEALTH THROUGH PREVENTION AND NON-MEDICAL SERVICES

There are many lifestyle and diet elements that research has shown can dramatically affect your overall health. Before, during, or after battling a major illness, maximizing your healthy behaviors can impact your need for, access to, and cost of care.

Medical research and the medical community suggest that individuals maintain an overall healthy lifestyle. Listed here are some of the topics for good health that are tied to lower illness rates and better overall health.

- Eat a well-rounded and balanced diet.
- Limit salt intake.
- Ensure you are getting proper vitamins, minerals, and nutrition.
- Stop smoking and tobacco use.
- Manage your stress level.
- Limit excessive alcohol intake.
- Maintain a healthy weight.
- Incorporate exercise and movement into your lifestyle.
- Protect yourself against germs.
- Seek preventative and early detection care.
- Get enough sleep.

For more detail on these and more tips and guidelines for building a healthy lifestyle, visit cdc.gov/HealthyLiving.

CPSIA information can be obtained at www.ICGtesting.com
Printed in the USA
BVOW08s1932011215

429039BV00003B/40/P

9 781633 931862